## BOOKS BY BRUCE TEGNER

BRUCE TEGNER'S COMPLETE BOOK OF SELF-DEFENSE:

BRUCE TEGNER'S COMPLETE BOOK OF KARATE

BRUCE TEGNER'S COMPLETE BOOK OF AIKIDO

BRUCE TEGNER'S COMPLETE BOOK OF JUKADO SELF-DEFENSE
Jiu Jitsu Modernized

BRUCE TEGNER'S COMPLETE BOOK OF JUDO

KARATE: Self-Defense & Traditional Sport Forms

KARATE & JUDO EXERCISES

STICK FIGHTING: SPORT FORMS

STICK FIGHTING: SELF-DEFENSE

DEFENSE TACTICS FOR LAW ENFORCEMENT:
Weaponless Defense & Control

SELF-DEFENSE NERVE CENTERS & PRESSURE POINTS

BRUCE TEGNER METHOD OF SELF-DEFENSE:
The Best of Judo, Jiu Jitsu, Karate, Yawara, etc.

SELF-DEFENSE FOR BOYS & MEN:
A Physical Education Course

SELF-DEFENSE YOU CAN TEACH YOUR BOY:
A Confidence-Building Course, Elementary School Age

SELF-DEFENSE FOR WOMEN: (With Alice McGrath)
A Simple Method for Home Study

SELF-DEFENSE FOR GIRLS & WOMEN: (With Alice McGrath)
A Physical Education Course

BLACK BELT JUDO, KARATE, JUKADO

AIKIDO and Jiu Jitsu Holds & Locks

JUDO FOR FUN: Sport Techniques

SAVATE: French Foot & Fist Fighting

KUNG FU & TAI CHI: Chinese Karate & Classical Exercise

Additional titles in preparation

# BRUCE TEGNER'S COMPLETE BOOK OF SELF-DEFENSE

COMPLETELY NEW EDITION



THOR PUBLISHING COMPANY

VENTURA, CALIFORNIA 93001

**Library of Congress Cataloging in Publication Data**

Tegner, Bruce.
Bruce Tegnér's complete book of self-defense.

Includes index.
1. Self-defense. I. Title. II. Title: Complete book of self-defense.
GV1111.T3864 796.8 74-28358
ISBN 0-87504-510-6

---

*In 1963, a book titled Bruce Tegner's Complete Book of Self-Defense was published by Stein & Day. The present book is completely new. All text in this edition is new, as are the photos; the material has been updated and reorganized.*

*First printing: April 1975*

ACKNOWLEDGMENTS: The author wishes to express appreciation to: Ray Coleman, Rocky Escalanti, Jeff Hager, Don Hairston, Holly Haverty, Marleen Haverty, Kelly McEnroe, Jean Windishar and Richard Windishar for demonstrating the techniques of self-defense.

BRUCE TEGNER'S COMPLETE BOOK OF SELF-DEFENSE
*Manuscript prepared under the supervision of*
*ALICE McGRATH*



THOR PUBLISHING COMPANY • P.O. BOX 1782
VENTURA CALIFORNIA 93001

PRINTED IN THE UNITED STATES OF AMERICA

## BRUCE TEGNER BOOKS REVIEWED

BRUCE TEGNER'S COMPLETE BOOK OF KARATE (2nd revised edition)

"... Tegner suggests and illustrates changes which would bring karate more in line with modern concepts of physical education ... invaluable as a guide to teaching karate in schools, colleges and recreation centers."

Dr. Ray Snyder, CAHPER

DEFENSE TACTICS FOR LAW ENFORCEMENT
Volume One: Weaponless Defense and Control

"... a comprehensive manual ... a practical tool applicable to police academy programs, pre-service police science programs at the university level and for the (individual) officer ..."

THE POLICE CHIEF

BRUCE TEGNER'S COMPLETE BOOK OF JUKADO SELF-DEFENSE: Jiu Jitsu Modernized

"This is the most useful book on the Oriental fighting arts that I have ever seen."

Michael H. Dygert, LIBRARY JOURNAL

SELF-DEFENSE YOU CAN TEACH YOUR BOY: A Confidence-Building Course (for elementary school age boys)

"The easy to learn defenses are safe and practical."

JOURNAL OF HEALTH, PHYSICAL EDUCATION and RECREATION

SELF-DEFENSE FOR GIRLS & WOMEN (with Alice McGrath, a physical education course for girls and women in secondary schools.)

"... The authors' advice is sound and their methods could easily be practiced in gym classes."

Charles Curran, LIBRARY JOURNAL

SELF-DEFENSE NERVE CENTERS & PRESSURE POINTS

"Students and teachers of unarmed fighting will find much valuable source material in this attractive book."

SCHOLASTIC COACH

SELF-DEFENSE FOR BOYS & MEN (A physical education course for secondary schools.)

"... recommended for school libraries. The text deserves inspection by physical education instructors."

Charles Curran, LIBRARY JOURNAL

KUNG FU & TAI CHI: Chinese Karate Forms and Classical Exercise

"... recommended for physical fitness collections."

Charles Curran, LIBRARY JOURNAL

# CONTENTS



## INTRODUCTION



## INSTRUCTION PART ONE



## PART TWO

## PART THREE



## PART FOUR



## PART FIVE



## PART SIX

## PREFACE

In response to the fear of assault, most people experience themselves as potential victims—as prey—or as potential predators. For most people neither role is acceptable. The role of victim is usually accompanied by feelings of shame and humiliation. If there has been a history of experiencing one's self as a victim, there is often an accompanying fantasy of revenge. Though it is romanticized in the media, the role of predator is repugnant to most of us.

So there we are—trapped between the terror of being a victim or the obsession of being a vengeful aggressor. We seem to be given the alternative of being feared or being fearful. The sense of helplessness which results from not having a satisfactory choice of roles is painful, confusing and frightening.

Mastery, control of one's life, means having a sense of alternatives from which acceptable choices can be made. The sense of being able to choose, and of having, to some degree, choices which are life-enhancing, can be arrived at in a number of ways, but it must be *experienced* as an internal state, not simply as an idea. When this state of grace is reached, we can face the fact that many of us are basically lovers and not fighters and can accept this without feeling humiliation and, instead, feel appropriate pride.

In my professional opinion, Bruce Tegner seems uncommonly aware of this psychically realistic frame of reference. He understands the support and confidence levels which are useful to people trying to work themselves out of the submission-vengeance trap. He really understands that mastery is not something you do to other people.

Because of his attitudes and his awareness of the problems with which so many people, and especially young people, must struggle, I highly recommend Bruce Tegner's approach to self-defense.

MARTIN BERKOWITZ, Ph.D., ABPP
Los Angeles, California

# INTRODUCTION

## SELF-DEFENSE: A Point of View

Almost anyone can learn practical self-defense in a fairly short period of time without becoming an expert fighter. This point of view is based on a lifetime of experience in the field.

The principal obstacle to learning and teaching practical self-defense is a persistence of concepts and practices which do not serve our present needs. It is time to examine and re-evaluate out-dated ideas on the subject of self-defense. It is imperative to apply rational, ethical, humanistic standards of behavior to this subject. It is necessary to apply modern concepts of education since the major consumers of books and instruction are young people.

A definition of self-defense is in order. One way of defining self-defense is to enumerate the things it is *not*. Self-defense is not warfare; it is not personal vengeance; it is not ritual or ceremony; it is not an art; it is not a sporting event; it is not a way of life; it is not a spectacular tv/movie fight scene.

Self-defense instruction is preparation to minimize the possibility of assault, to minimize the possibility of engaging in physical confrontation; it is training to learn and use a group of simple, effective physical actions if no other alternative is available. Learning self-defense is primarily the process of learning how to avoid being a victim.

For a long time we have been exposed to either/or, all-or-none fallacies about self-defense. It is still widely believed that the alternative to becoming a highly trained fighter is to be a completely helpless person, unable to cope with the threat of assault. Put another way, it is a statement that the only alternative to passivity is aggression. There is, in fact, another possibility. The rational alternative to aggression is not submission, but assertion.

Many victims of assault are not victims because they fail to become fierce fighters; they are victims of assault because they have been given *no* preparation to deal with this special kind of emergency. The view that self-defense instruction is preparation to become a skilled fighter has the effect of eliminating those individuals who most need to know self-defense. It is precisely those individuals who are unable or unwilling to become expert fighters who benefit from practical self-defense instruction to the greatest degree.

Our capabilities ought to bear some relationship to real-life objectives. People learning to defend themselves against assault ought *not* to be trained as though they were preparing for warfare. In warfare the objective is to inflict grave injury or to kill an adversary. The legal and moral definition of self-defense expressly limits the degree or amount of force to the *least* amount which can be used to avert or stop an intended assault. Warfare training is preparation to use the *maximum* degree of force.

The concepts, techniques and methods appropriate for training Samurai warriors are not those appropriate for teaching self-defense as a practical skill.

Punitive responses to violence do not contribute solutions —they escalate violence. Community safety is a community problem. Safe streets will not be achieved through reckless counter-aggression. The "harder" we come down on individuals who resort to physical assault, the more we seem to convince them that violence is a legitimate form of persuasion. Personal vengeance is not consistent with protection under the law. It is understandable that individuals take violent action when they are severely frustrated, but personal vengeance destroys the law, just as kicking a tv set because it doesn't work destroys the possibility that it might be made to work. Personal vengeance is a dramatic theme for plays and stories, but the outcome of personal vengeance is always tragic.

Street assault is not a sporting event and self-defense is not a sport. A sport has rules, regulations, judges, referees. Opponents in a sporting match are expected to be of approximately equal size and weight and to have approximately equal skill. In a sporting match the participants have a mutual agreement to engage in contest and they have agreed to abide by a set of known rules.

The objectives of a sporting match are demonstrably different from the objectives of street assault or street defense. The method of instruction, the techniques selected, the amount of training and practice are different for tournament and for basic self-defense. Preparation for tournament requires hard work, long training, exercise to get into top physical condition, continuing practice to maintain a high level of technical skill and a competitive spirit. Such requirements are appropriate for sport training and they are utterly without relevance for practical self-defense. Contest-oriented training ignores those most urgently in need of self-defense instruction—the frail, those who are not competitive, those who are not in superb physical condition, those who are not exceptional in physical performance.

Many forms of the ancient fighting skills, the martial arts of Asia, include rigid patterns of "attack-defense" exercises which originated as practice procedures to enhance technical skill. Through the years, they have evolved into ritualized, formal movements, some of which bear no relationship to defense actions which would be appropriate in contemporary assault-defense situations. The ritual and formal aspects of the fighting skills bear about the same relationship to practical self-defense as the tea ceremony has to making a cup of tea. There is no doubt but what the tea ceremony is one of the most beautiful patterns of formal ceremony in the world, but no one would claim that it is the most efficient way to brew a cup of tea for everyday consumption.

Calling self-defense an "art" is, in my view, counterproductive. Self-defense is a practical skill which ought to be available to great numbers of ordinary people. "Art" implies aptitudes, gifts, talents and accomplishments which are beyond the reach of most of us. Even when the word "art" is used to describe a craft, it is applied to those who have exceptional ability. Self-defense is a practical skill which most people can learn.

It used to be alleged that judo is a "way of life." Now that judo is an Olympic Games event, it is clear that judo is a "way of life" only in the sense that swimming is a "way of life" for an individual who expects to become an Olympic champion. Champions must devote the major part of their lives to learning and practicing the activity in order to excel. The individual who wants to learn the fundamentals of swimming as a safety skill and for pleasurable exercise does not need to make swimming a "way of life." The person who wishes to reach a high level of skill in any weaponless fighting specialty must devote much time, attention and energy to reach that goal. The person who wishes to learn basic self-defense need not.

Finally, self-defense does not bear any relationship to fighting that you see on the screen.

## FIGHTING IN FILMS

Every fight scene in a movie is planned, move by move, blow by blow. Whether or not the actors in tv shows and films have any fighting skill is irrelevant. Fight scenes are played by actors who are paid to act the roles of villains and the roles of heroes. The heroes do not win movie fights because they can fight better than the villains, but because the script tells them when to win and when to lose. Even when actors do have fighting skill, the story determines what they are going to do and how to do it.

Films and tv shows are not made to instruct us but to amaze and entertain us. Off-stage trampolines are used so that actors can leap higher into the air than any human could do in real life. Stunt men are paid to tumble and fall in a way that makes it appear they have sustained forceful blows. Villains carefully stay out of the way of the hero until it is their turn to be chopped, stabbed or leaped at.

In my long experience working in films, I have often had the job of training the hero to play a fight scene which I have designed; then I have worked with stunt men, coaching them to lose the fight in the most spectacular manner; then I have played the role of a villain, "losing" the fight to the hero whom I had taught to "win" the fight. There are actors whose skills at learning fight techniques are superior. Rick Nelson and James Coburn are among the actors I have worked with whose ability to learn and perform in fight scenes is really outstanding. Nevertheless, in the films where these talents were used, the fight scene itself was carefully planned, rehearsed over and over, and filmed according to the script. This is what makes film fighting different from a street defense. In the movies, if the actor performs the dazzling and difficult fighting technique less than perfectly, they shoot the scene over. So, no matter what style of fighting is shown, or what the circumstances of the fight scene, the hero wins when he ought to and loses when the plot reads that way. This explains why the style of fighting in the movies is of no consequence and of no particular value as a guide to practical self-defense.

### WHAT KIND OF SELF-DEFENSE IS THIS?

The defenses in this book are more closely related to jiu jitsu than to any other form of weaponless fighting.

All fighting techniques can be described in a few main categories. There are fewer styles of weaponless fighting than you might imagine from hearing so many exotic names for them. Although there are subtle stylistic variations among them, all forms of karate and kung fu are essentially hand and foot blows. All forms of kung fu and karate have more elements in common than they have differences. But karate and kung fu are different from judo because judo is the skill of throwing and grappling, rather than the skill of hitting and kicking. And aikido is different from judo and kung fu, because aikido techniques are based on twisting and bending joints.

Jiu jitsu (there are dozens and dozens of "styles" of jiu jitsu) is essentially a combination of techniques taken from the various categories of fighting: there are hand and foot blows, there are trips and takedowns, there are twisting and bending of joints, which we also call holds and locks, and there are escapes. Jiu jitsu is more versatile than a single specialty, covers a wider range of material than kung fu, or karate, or judo or aikido, and includes many techniques which are common to the specialties.

The major difference between my adaptation of jiu jitsu for modern self-defense and the traditional forms of jiu jitsu is that I have eliminated the concept of teaching a separate, specific defense for every separate specific attack. Instead, I have introduced the concept of a small group of defense actions which make up the basic "vocabulary" of practical defense. With these techniques in various, flexible combinations it is possible to defend against a great number of common assaults without having to commit to memory hundreds of rigid defense "tricks."

If you were to learn only ten defense actions and know them well, you would have available to you, literally, thousands of different combinations for practical defense. It is very difficult to recall specific series of actions without constant, ongoing practice, but it is not difficult to remember ten actions and apply them in any combination which is possible and appropriate.

Imagine that you know ten defense actions well enough to use them without undue hesitation. Then imagine that you use only four of these actions at any one time, in different combinations; the possible combinations you could make would be 5,040! Think how long it would take to learn five *hundred* to say nothing of how long it would take to learn five thousand specific defenses and you will understand the advantage of learning flexible, rather than rigid series of defense actions.

There are some defenses which are taught as specific responses to specific assaults, but as you learn them, you will also learn procedures for minimizing the possibility of having to deal with them as completed assaults. Stopping an intended assault is as important as, or more important than, learning to defend after the assault has been completed. In this, too, my approach is different from the old-fashioned jiu jitsu training procedures which are always practiced as though an intended assault must be completed before the defense begins.

Finally, I have eliminated techniques and practice procedures which have no application to modern life. Old-fashioned jiu jitsu methods still include defenses against kneeling sword attacks, for instance, because such defenses were incorporated into the system long ago and have become traditional. I have modified, adapted, simplified and rationalized as necessary to make the system work for people's needs, rather than trying to make people adapt themselves to an outdated system.

### YOUR SECRET POWER

The element of surprise works in your favor for self-defense. If you have to use the physical actions, don't give away your advantage by telling your assailant what you are going to do. Unexpectedness is disconcerting and confusing.

If you are working to gain self-confidence and self-assertion, don't talk about your self-defense practice. Self-defense actions should be kept a secret so that you have the advantage of surprise should you need to use it, but also because it is most effective as a source of inner power.

Furthermore, self-defense does not come off effectively as a demonstration to a friend. If you try to demonstrate that you know self-defense, you are, in effect, challenging your friend. Then, when you attempt to demonstrate what you can do, your friend will make his attack as realistic as he can, but you cannot make your defense realistic. You are not going to kick a friend's shin with vigor, just to show that you can defend yourself. The result of trying to "prove" self-defense to friends and acquaintances is disappointing and negative. If you did the defense vigorously and with spirit, it would be effective. Simulating the defense is perfectly appropriate for learning self-defense, but not a very satisfactory way of "proving" that you can defend yourself. It is more prudent and useful and tactically shrewd to keep your self-defense ability a quiet source of back-up for assertive behavior that can minimize the possibility of assault.

## ASSERTIVE BEHAVIOR EQUALS CONFIDENCE

What pleases me most about the students who have studied with me or followed my method of teaching, is not that they can beat up on assailants, but that they have the composure to cope with threatening situations so that very few of them have to resort to physical action. When they do, they are successful within my definition of self-defense—they can stop the intended assault and escape from it with a minimum of force. They win, but it is not a triumph of physical power as much as it is an assertion of control—of self-control.

It is not scientifically accurate to assign simple categories of human behavior, because most of us are complicated individuals who behave in complex ways, some of them contradictory, in different roles and different situations. For our present purpose, however, it is useful to think of the possible reactions to the threat of assault as falling into three main categories—passive, aggressive and assertive.

The passive response to the threat of assault, for the most part, encourages the assailant by assuring him that no effort will be made to stop his intended assault. Since an assailant usually chooses a victim, rather than an adversary, submissive behavior validates his choice—it tells him he has assigned the role of victim to an individual who will accept that role without protest.

Victims are unwitting accomplices to their assailants by showing helplessness and panic. When the intended victim refuses to play the role of victim, it is disconcerting to the aggressor. The assailant who threatens a smaller or seemingly helpless person is not brave. A show of willingness to avoid being a victim is often enough to prevent assault.

An aggressive reaction to the possibility of assault is evidenced in a willingness or desire to use as much or more force than is threatened. When greater force is used than is necessary to stop the intended assault, that is not self-defense, it is punishment. Under a government of law, individuals do not have the legal or moral right to punish. There is a great deal of aggression inherent in presenting self-defense as a way of "teaching a lesson" to the assailant. This approach validates violence and it brutalizes the individuals who accept the premise.

There is a third kind of behavior which is neither the passivity of the victim nor the aggressiveness of the bully; it is self-reliant assertiveness.

A victim permits others to manipulate his or her behavior. An aggressor tries to manipulate the behavior of others. The assertive person refuses to be taken advantage of and refuses to take advantage of other people. The always-passive person loses control through not acting. The aggressive person loses control through inappropriate action. The assertive person, through conscious self-control, has the greatest degree of freedom from control by others.

Becoming an assertive person is a process. There is no secret formula or magic phrase which changes people from being submissive, passive individuals to self-confident, assertive persons.

Most behavior is learned. When submissive behavior has become habitual, it takes un-learning and re-learning to acquire the attitudes, responses, gestures and language appropriate to assertive behavior. Learning self-defense can be a beginning. Once you realize that you need not be a victim of assault through passive, helpless behavior, that realization can help you make a conscious shift in your attitude toward yourself. Assertive behavior in daily life will enhance your self-defense capability and will help release your potential for self-development, self-actualization and self-regard.

**THE IRVING INCIDENT**

Positive action does not always mean that you have to hit the aggressive individual who is bothering you. There is, in many, many situations, the option of taking control without touching your "adversary."

Irving (not his real name, though this is a true story) was a student in middle age, of unimposing appearance, of more than average intelligence and with less than average talent for learning body skills. He came to my school in Hollywood saying that he wanted to learn karate for exercise. He attended classes faithfully and made moderately good progress, considering everything. After having practiced for some months, he decided to take the classes of practical defense instead of continuing sport karate. In all, he attended classes for almost a year. At the end of the year he had a purple belt in karate and he had learned the fundamentals of practical defense. Not a dazzling record.

One evening Irving came to class beaming. He confessed to his original reason for coming to take lessons. For years he had been subjected to a peculiarly humiliating action—one which he felt helpless to correct or to cope with. He belonged to a social club. A very large, hearty, obnoxious member of that club took delight in whacking Irving on the back and then rubbing Irving's bald head, making some joking remark about bald Irving. That was all. That was the extent of the aggression. There was no question of being physically harmed or injured. Still, Irving felt demeaned, frustrated and angry—and helpless! Irving explained that he had been taking first karate lessons and then self-defense lessons in the expectation of learning a physical action with which to retaliate against his tormentor. He had switched from karate to practical self-defense when he realized that, even if he could learn karate, it was not appropriate. A leaping kick (even if he could do it) or a smashing fist blow against an annoying person is an obvious over-reaction. Irving felt that the simple techniques of practical self-defense were more suited to his purpose and he looked forward to the time when he could put a stop to his recurring humiliation.

And finally he did. The evening before Irving told me this story he went to the club meeting. The hearty bully whacked Irving on the back and started to rub Irving's head. Irving backed away from him and said: "I wish you wouldn't do that to me. I don't like it." The other man said: "Oh, I'm sorry. I didn't mean to offend you."

That's all there is to the Irving incident.

Irving told me that it had been one of the happiest moments of his life. He felt that he was no longer a person who could be victimized and humiliated. He felt that he could stand up for himself. He expressed pleasure that he had not had to use any physical force to win his quiet battle.

We talked about this incident for a long time. I asked Irving why he had never before thought of simply asking the man to stop this offensive behavior. Irving told me that he thought that somehow if he mentioned it, it would get worse. That if he objected, it would make his tormentor more aggressive. And then he said, "If he hurt me, I wouldn't know what to do."

It took Irving longer than most to gather his inner strength to behave in an affirmative way. It had taken him longer than many to learn that the alternative to passivity is not necessarily counter-aggression. And he needed the support of knowing the physical actions of self-defense in order to assert himself.

Irving realized, finally, that he had not been a victim of the bully, but that he had been a victim of his own timidity. His diffident attitude had encouraged aggressive behavior. He realized, too, that counter-aggressive behavior would have triggered off a chain of events that he might not be able to control, and that a hostile response would have been unproductive. He was, after that evening, more relaxed, more composed. Most important, he felt a renewed sense of self-esteem because he had acted in a rational, mature way.

There are many people who never learn the physical actions of self-defense who, nevertheless, are perfectly able to take care of themselves. These are the people who have grown up assertive, whose pattern of behavior has become obviously non-passive so that they do not offer themselves as targets for aggression. They radiate a sense of self-assurance which is entirely different from the *machismo* of hostility. But there are many others who need to learn the physical actions of self-defense to give them a sense of security so that they can behave in a non-violent, non-hostile, assertive way. It is for these people that I am writing. It is a source of great satisfaction to me that my approach and my methods are helping people escape the confining restrictions of their own passivity without encouraging aggression as an alternative.

Not everyone can fight a bull barehanded. But almost anyone can make progress from a state of helplessness to a state of competent self-sufficiency.

Better than any number of boards broken, or blocks of ice smashed, or movie stories of violent vengeance, the Irving incident illustrates the possibilities of significant personal growth toward maturity and dignity.

### HAND CONDITIONING: A Warning

There is no need to condition your hands for either sport or self-defense fighting skills. Hand conditioning is a process of hardening and desensitizing the hands. Individuals with heavily conditioned hands can do sensational breaking tricks and they can hit hard surfaces with full-power blows without hurting themselves, for they have lost the ability to feel pain. Extreme conditioning is called the "iron hand" and I have personally witnessed an individual whose knuckles were so conditioned that he could drive a nail into wood using his bare hand.

The process of hand conditioning had a function in the past. When karate fighters had to break through wooden armor, they needed to make weapons of their hands. When karate was intended for hand-to-hand combat with the objective of killing the enemy, karate fighters had to spend years hitting at trees to prepare for battle.

Extreme conditioning can seriously impair manual dexterity and the disability is permanent. Once you lose the ability to do intricate, delicate movements with your hands because of extreme hand conditioning, you cannot regain it. Conditioned hands are unattractive and an impediment to job acceptance. If you ever expect to work where you have to meet the public in any capacity, conditioned hands could mean a loss of that opportunity.

In addition to the physical disability and the ugliness, I have a further objection to hand conditioning. It is inappropriate.

In sport karate, the players are not permitted to make contact, thus, conditioned hands have absolutely no function.

For self-defense, conditioned hands could be an impediment rather than an asset. If self-defense is viewed (as I view it) as preparation to avoid fighting and to use the least amount of force if one has to fight, how is it possible to reconcile heavily conditioned hands with that objective? If one gives the appearance of preparing to fight, by conditioning the hands, it is difficult to maintain the role of self-defender; conditioned hands give the appearance of preparation for aggression.

Since the great majority of you reading my books are young people, I would particularly warn you against hand conditioning. The youthful indiscretion of hand conditioning can be regretted, but it cannot be undone.

## COLORED BELTS

The ancient forms of weaponless fighting did not award belt degrees, wear special uniforms or engage in contest. Judo was the first of the Asian specialties of hand-to-hand combat to be modified and adapted for modern sport with the objective of physical development. With its conversion to sport and physical education uses, judo players were ranked according to skill in competition and demonstration of formal technique. Contrary to popular belief, the first black belt holders were not deadly killers; they were skilled sportsmen.

The myth of the black belt has spread widely and many people are convinced that the wearer of a black belt has super-human powers, that only a black belt qualifies a teacher of self-defense, that one must have a colored belt to validate self-defense skills, and so on, through a long list of erroneous information about belt ranking.

The colored belts of judo, karate and of other weaponless fighting, are awarded primarily for contest skill or for performance of rehearsed routines. Since no school or style of any of the fighting skills awards belts in the same manner and since no school or style acknowledges the validity of a colored belt earned in any other school or style, the colored belt ranks have significance only in the school or system in which they are awarded.

Self-defense can be learned without ranks or colored belts. The requirement of working toward belt ranks as a prerequisite for learning self-defense, is, in my view, an impediment to teaching and learning practical self-defense.

According to the school of thought which insists on colored belt ranking as a prerequisite for learning "self-defense" every little old lady would have to become a black belt holder in order to learn to cope with assault. How unrealistic! According to the skill-through-contest school of thought, every little old lady would have to enter tournament in order to protect herself. If that sounds exaggerated, think about it carefully. Who is more vulnerable to assault—a little old lady or a strong young athlete? The obvious conclusion must be that those most vulnerable to assault must be taught effective means of coping with it and that working toward colored belt degrees must not be confused with learning practical self-defense.

**GUNS FOR SELF-DEFENSE?**

In my view, there are practical, ethical and psychological arguments against owning handguns for self-defense which far outweigh any possible advantage.

There are some special instances, professionals in law enforcement and individuals living in remote, isolated areas, for instance, in which guns might be the appropriate protection. But my reasons and arguments apply to the general public—to the person who has or is considering owning a gun for personal defense.

A gun, or any other weapon, is not adequate protection unless it is carried at all times. The alternative to carrying it on your person at all times is to have it easily accessible to you at all times. If it is easily accessible to you, it is easily accessible to others, including children.

In practice and in fact, the guns which are bought for "self-defense" are used to kill children, wives, lovers, husbands, parents and neighbors far more frequently than they are used to kill criminals. Of the annual shooting deaths which occur in the United States, a majority are murders of rage or accidental killings; a small number are termed justifiable. The slogan which implies that people are responsible for murder and that the murder would occur without the weapon is a distortion of the facts. Children who shoot their brothers in a fit of rage or by accident would not commit murder by other means.

A community which values the concept of law and order cannot condone the unregulated, widespread ownership of handguns. The alternatives are not the control of guns *or* the control of criminals; our communities must learn to control both. The advocates of uncontrolled gun ownership have made it seem that legislation regulating the sale and ownership of handguns is controversial and would somehow favor criminals. Reliable opinion polls indicate that the majority of us believe that effective gun controls should be put into effect. For the evidence strongly suggests that we are in grave danger of violence from ordinary citizens who carry guns.

Anyone who kills, even in self-defense, has to live with the consequences of that action for a life-time. Killing, even in self-defense, must ordinarily be justified through a trial in court. This is proper, otherwise we would be giving up our own rights. If you were the victim of gun assault by someone who hated you, you would be outraged if he could avoid the consequences of his action by using the phrase "self-defense" to avoid legal action.

Professionals in law enforcement are increasingly in favor of controls for civilian handgun ownership. Police officers are more in danger of being shot when responding to family disputes than they are when dealing with professional criminals.

Article II of the U.S. Constitution begins with the words "A well-regulated militia . . ." The "right" to bear arms free of control is not guaranteed by the Constitution. The "right" to bear arms for personal vengeance is not a "right." The right to hold unpopular opinions and exchange views freely is a condition of the freedom to live freely in a free society. It is one of the basic rights. There is no such "right" as the "right" to kill.

**HOW TO USE THE BOOK**

Before you begin to practice techniques, read the introductory material with care. Glance at the photos and look through the text superficially—just enough to become acquainted with the ideas and the scope of the instruction. Pay special attention to the information dealing with safety in practice.

Refer to the lesson plans for guidance.

When you begin to practice the defense actions, reread the text carefully. Study the photos so that you are thoroughly familiar with the gesture and movement of each action.

If you are in a negotiating relationship, trying to cool down a threatening individual, you would certainly not start with a startling yell, though you should be prepared to use it if he makes a move to assault. Yelling is an aid in those instances when you are past the point of talking. Screaming is not appropriate for situations in which you need a subtle distraction, rather than a dramatic, startling action. As you proceed through the text, you should be able to determine which kinds of situations indicate that subtle gestures of distraction would help your defense and in which situations a dramatic, startling, whooping yell would be useful and appropriate.

## SAFETY IN PRACTICE

There is no need for either partner to be hurt during practice of self-defense techniques. The practice sessions are not for the purpose of *proving* the techniques, but for the purpose of learning them and rehearsing them.

Use your imagination. You know that if you were kicked in the shin, vigorously, you would feel considerable pain. But when you are practicing how to kick into the shin, you simulate the action. You do not really kick your partner in the shin. Your gesture, your expression, your body and leg movement can be realistically forceful—but you are careful not to make contact.

When you are learning the ways of hitting and kicking, you may touch your partner *very lightly,* just to feel the proper position and relationship. When you are instructed to hit your partner, it always means that you simulate a hit. Contact hitting and kicking may be done with training aids, not against your partner.

Highly trained individuals can deliver fast and forceful hand and foot blows to within an inch of the intended target without touching it; training and practice is required for such control. Individuals who are learning practical self-defense will insure safe practice by aiming their simulated blows at least six inches away from the partner's body target area.

## TAPPING FOR SAFETY

The best procedure for telling your partner "stop" or "let go" is the tapping signal. You can tap him with your open hand, a very light slapping action, or you can tap yourself. Before you practice any of the defenses, rehearse tapping. If your partner grips your arm, tap his gripping arm lightly as the signal to let go. The partner who is tapped must release instantly. If your partner grips your body from behind, pinning your arms, tap your own leg. The partner who is gripping must release instantly upon hearing the tapping signal. Further along in the instruction you will realize why the tapping signal is essential for good, safe practice.

If you are practicing the chokes, for instance, and your partner grips too realistically, you can tap for release. If your partner grips or grabs or holds you in a rough or careless manner, tap to indicate "stop" and tell him to start over. It is reckless to work with a partner who does not release upon the tapping signal; it is unproductive to work with a partner who is consistently rough; it is foolish to work with a partner who does not follow the rules of safety in practice.

In any kind of body contact physical activity, the principal cause of accident is: Failure to observe the stated rules of safety, through inattention or kidding around. A prime rule of safety in practice is: DON'T FOOL AROUND!! Self-defense is not a game; it is a serious, practical skill.

## WORK SLOWLY

Working slowly is a precautionary procedure and a good learning method. It is much more important to learn the correct gesture and action of the defense techniques than it is to move fast. Particularly in the beginning, you will learn better if you pace your actions to your ability. A technique which you learn properly can be speeded up as you progress. Speed of execution, in any case, is not as important as you might think. During your training period, you might develop the ability to perform the defense actions with considerable speed; if you do not continue to practice, you will lose that ability. It is more important, if self-defense is to stay with you as a life-long skill, that you learn to perform the defense actions with a determined manner, serious expression, and an inner conviction of self-reliance.

Working slowly, you can concentrate on the two essential elements of practical self-defense—you can learn the proper action and you can rehearse the appropriate attitude.

## YELL & SCREAM

Yelling and screaming are splendid aids for defense actions. Loud yelling has several advantageous effects. In spite of the newspaper stories to the contrary, there is the possibility that screaming might attract help. Screaming is disconcerting to the assailant. Since most assailants attack with the expectation that the intended victim will not respond in a positive manner, screaming is excellent and unexpected behavior.

Screaming gives you a feeling of courage; it makes you feel determined. Within reasonable bounds, in appropriate ways, practice screaming and yelling with your defense actions. Most of us have no experience doing this and you and your partner will have to take turns playing the assailant role and the defender role. Yell directly at your partner. Scream as loud as you can and make it *look* as well as sound convincing.

There is an exception to the use of yelling for self-defense and it will be explained in the material relating to how to cope with the threat of armed assault.

# PART ONE

## HAND BLOWS

Hand blows for self-defense must not rely on the development of an exceptional degree of power, nor must they rely on an exceptional degree of accuracy or speed. Practical hand blows for self-defense are those which the average person can use without having years of training and without engaging in constant practice to maintain proficiency.

The body targets selected for practical self-defense must be appropriate. Finally, the types of hand blows should cover the possible range of situations from annoying to moderately serious to vicious assault. A mildly annoying situation should not be treated as though it were serious assault; the appropriate response to a vicious assault is different from the response to a humiliating, but not dangerous, aggressive action.

Of itself, a technique cannot be described as either moderate or forceful, with a few exceptions; poking fingers into the eye of an adversary, for example, is an extreme remedy, appropriate only for defense against vicious assault. Most of the other hand blows can be used in a manner ranging from mildly deterrent, through moderately vigorous to forceful. For practical self-defense I have eliminated those blows which are effective only if they are used by a highly trained individual or which require exceptional ability. I have selected the hand blows which most people can learn with relative ease and use efficiently after a moderate amount of practice.

## OPEN-HAND BLOWS

### Edge-of-Hand

A blow struck with the side of the hand is a highly efficient, flexible, advantageous technique for self-defense.

At one time this was called the jiu jitsu chop; later it was known as the judo chop, then it was identified as the karate chop and the kung fu chop. This hand blow has been given so many fancy names that it is impossible to list them all. They include: the knife-hand blow, the thousand-hand blow, the butterfly blow, the sword-hand blow and so on. It is the same blow, regardless of what it is called.

The edge-of-hand blow is delivered with a choppy action —with immediate recoil upon hitting the target. The manner of striking this blow resembles the correct way of hitting with a hammer; instead of a smashing, pile-driving effect, there is a bounce-back effect.

With your hand very slightly cupped, strike with the fleshy part of your palm, avoiding striking with any bony surface. You can determine the exact striking area by hitting lightly onto a hard surface, such as a table top, positioning your hand so that you can hit with moderate force without feeling pain. One of the great virtues of this technique is that you should be able to strike a full-force blow without hurting yourself. If you hit correctly, you can release all the power you are capable of delivering, without danger of injury to your hand.

It is not necessary to condition or callus your hand in order to use this blow effectively for practical self-defense.

1. The edge-of-hand blow can be delivered downward, as shown in this photo . . .

2. . . . or upward . . .

3. . . . or outward . . .

4. . . . or palm up.

Either hand can be used.

You will probably note a definite tendency to use only your strong hand in practice of the hand blows. Overcome that tendency by deliberately alternating right and left hands frequently. In street use, you would prefer to use your strong hand, but you must be prepared to use your weaker hand efficiently if your strong hand is gripped or captured. You must not rely on the most favorable circumstance in which to use self-defense techniques.

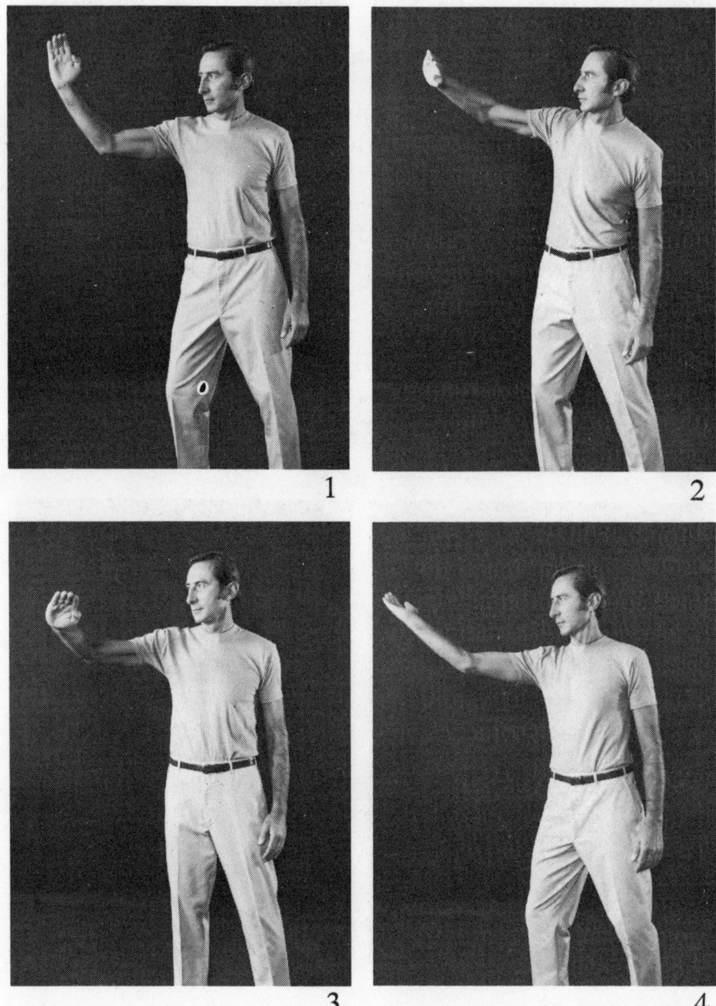

1 2

3 4

**TARGETS for Edge-of-Hand-Blows.**

The advantage of using an open hand blow is that you can hit or parry with it without coming into fist-hitting range of your adversary. If you can possibly avoid coming in close, you should do so.

We are so conditioned to move in closer to an adversary in order to deal with him, that it takes conscious effort and practice to overcome the habit. Step *away* from your adversary whenever it is appropriate and possible. If you come in close to hit him, you are placing yourself in hitting range.

The best arm targets you can hit, without getting within striking distance of your adversary's hand, are: wrist, forearm and into the bend of the elbow.

5. Hit at the wrist with a snappy, thrusting action to divert the intended blow, downward . . .

6. . . . or outward.

7. If you extend your arm fully, palm down, you will see a pronounced mound on your forearm just below your elbow. At this mound there is a vulnerable area which can be struck with the edge-of-hand blow . . .

5

6

8. . . . using either hand for striking.

9. Hitting into the inside of the forearm with the open hand blow can be done with either hand.

10. Striking into the bend of the elbow can be done with moderate ease, cross-body.

7

8

9

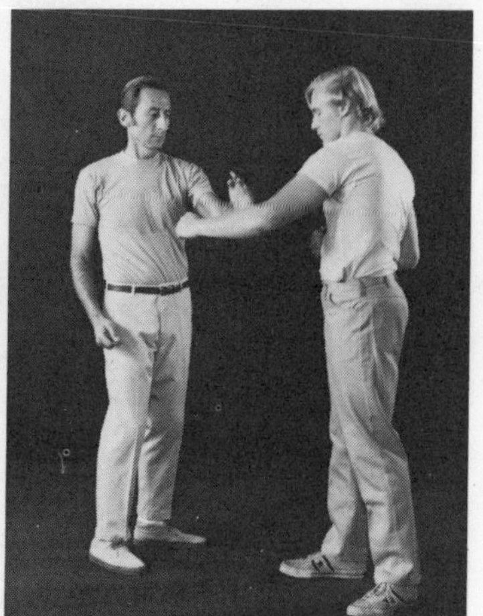

10

Hitting at the wrist has the virtue of diverting an intended blow; hitting onto the mound of the forearm results in pain —if the blow is struck with force, it can numb the arm briefly.

Hitting targets which can only be reached close in, putting you within your adversary's hitting range, should be reserved for those situations in which you are already in close and cannot move away, or when it is appropriate to the circumstance. In the event of serious assault you would not, by choice, step in close to your assailant if you could avoid doing so.

11. Strike with the edge-of-the-hand blow palm up, into the side of the neck.

12. Or, strike into the side of the neck back-handed, palm down.

13. Or, use both hands simultaneously to strike into both sides of the neck.

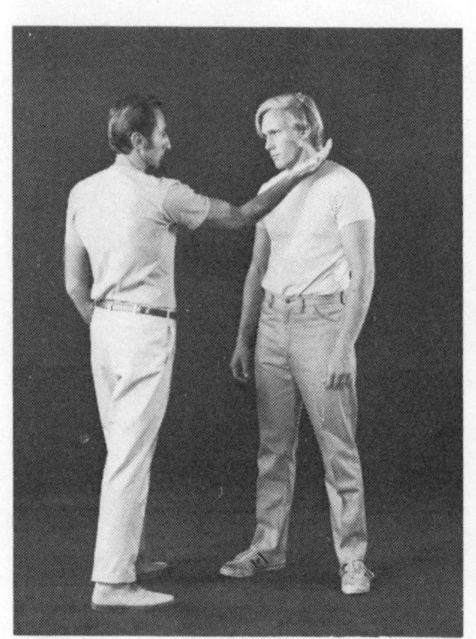

11

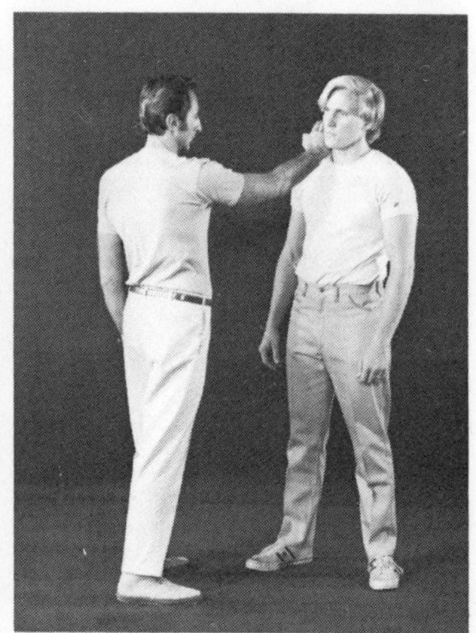

12

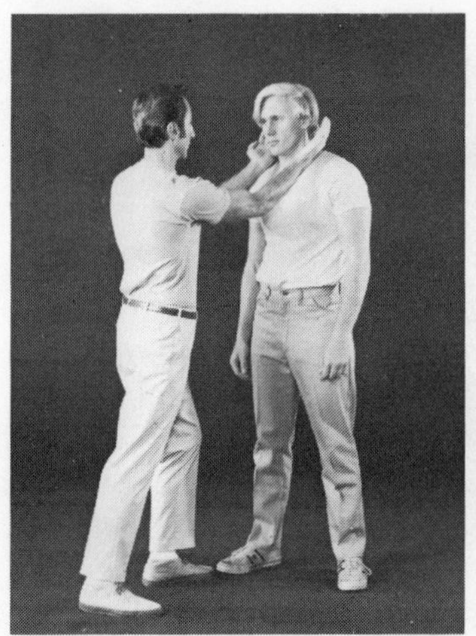

13

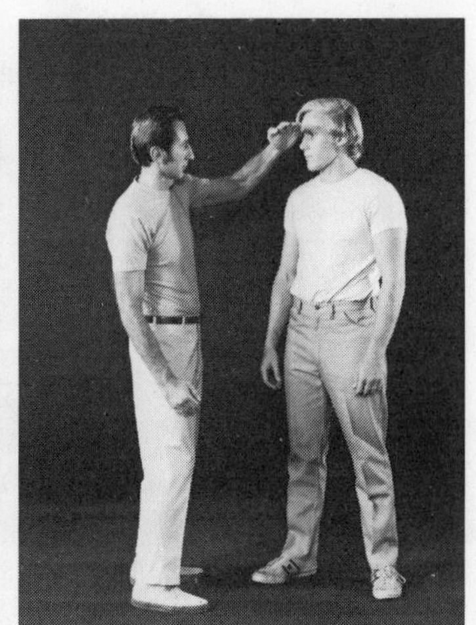

14

**14.** Strike sharply down onto the top of the nose, at the bridge.

**15.** Hit upward under the nose, back-handed.

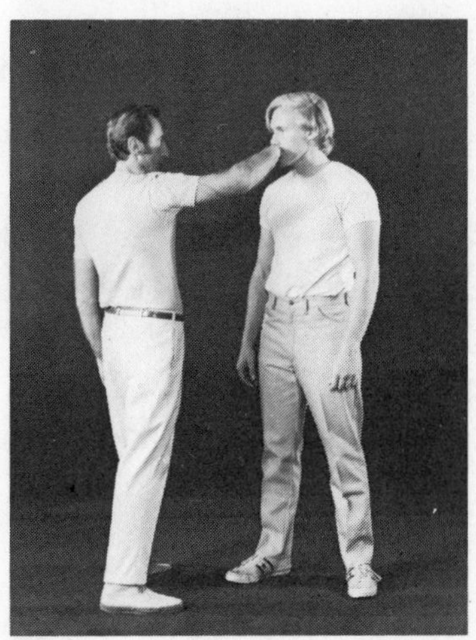

15

Hitting into the side of the neck is effective for self-defense and it is not a high-risk-of-injury tactic. If you hit with moderate force, it is painful and disorienting. A smaller person defending against a larger assailant would be unlikely to deliver the degree of power which could render an assailant unconscious.

Hitting onto the nose causes disorientation and pain. Hitting upward, under the nose, does *not* involve danger of "driving the nose bone into the brain." The nasal bones are considerably more fragile than the skull; the only skull opening above the nose is a tiny aperture; the nasal bones would have to be ground to a powder in order to enter through it. The notion that hitting up under the nose is a "fatal" blow derives from an ignorance of anatomy.

Hitting into the head, at any target point, may involve danger of injury if the force of the blow is great. The danger of injury from a blow to the head is a function of force, not a function of the type of blow or the exact target hit.

Hitting up under the nose is an excellent self-defense tactic, not because it is a "deadly" blow, but because it results in pain and disorientation.

16. Striking at an assailant behind you, can use the edge-of-hand blow upward . . .

17. . . . or downward onto his reaching arm, or . . .

18. . . . you can strike into the side of his neck.

19. The same blow can be used if you are behind him.

This would be an appropriate technique to complete a defense during which you deliberately place yourself behind your assailant. Examples of the use of this technique will be found further along in the book.

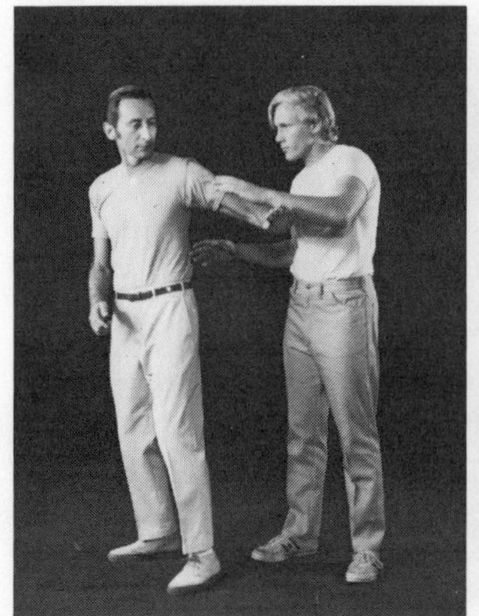

16

17

18

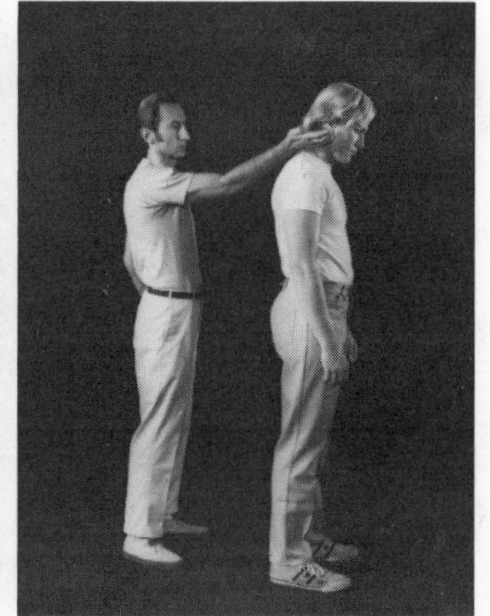

19

**HOW TO STRIKE**

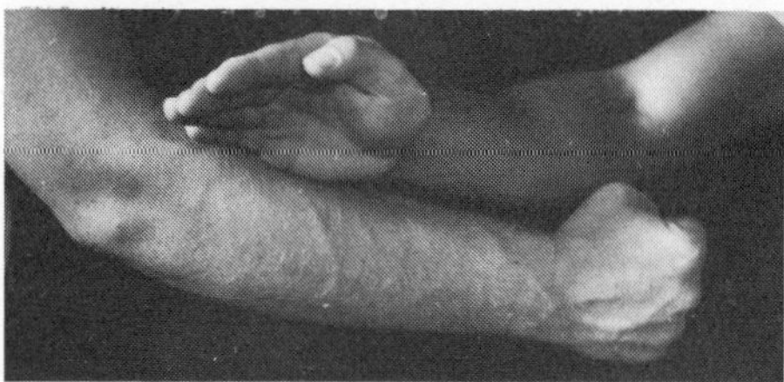

20. This close-up shows the correct position for the open-hand slash. Note that the hand is slightly cupped and the striking point is at the fleshy part of the palm.

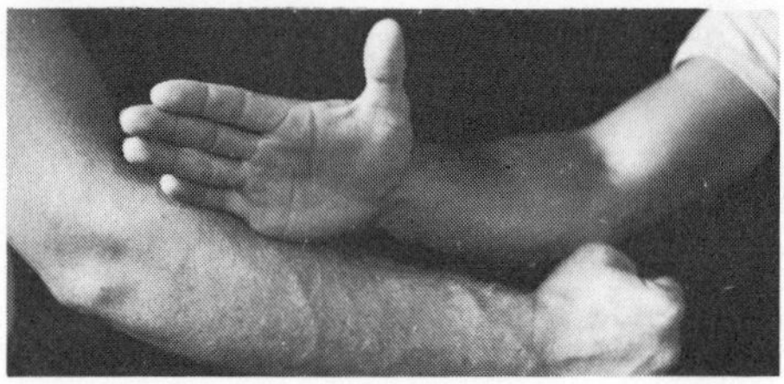

21. Avoid this error: Do not hold your thumb up; it should be held as in photo 20. Holding your thumb up decreases efficiency.

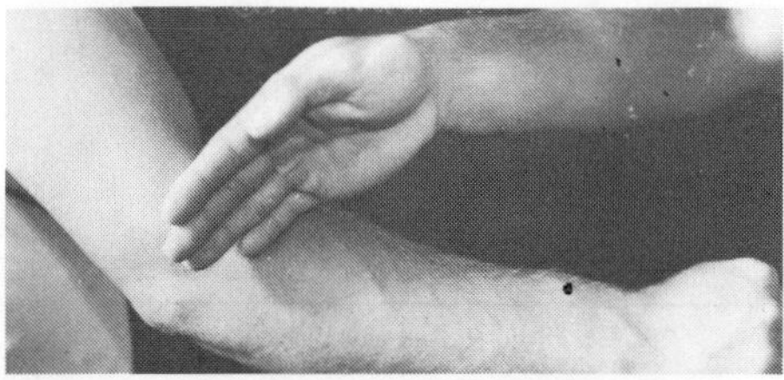

22. Avoid hitting onto your fingers.

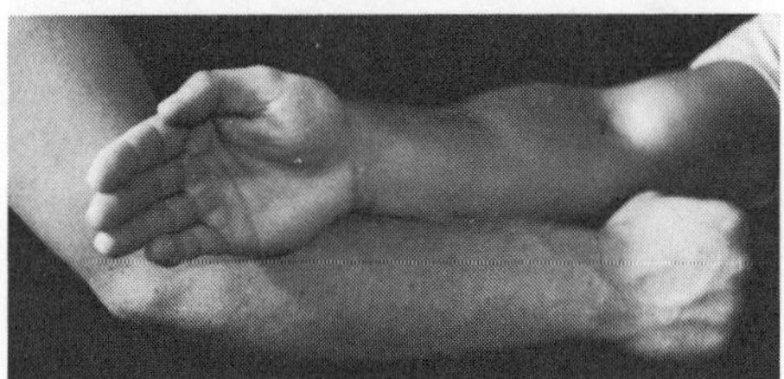

23. Avoid hitting with your wrist.

Begin slowly and cautiously. Hit lightly onto the hard surface and proceed to increase the force of your blow only as you determine that you are doing it correctly. If you feel bone contact, adjust the hand position to avoid that mistake. If your hand is tipped forward, as in photo 22, you will feel your little finger bone making contact with the surface; if you angle your hand too far upward, photo 23, you will feel your wrist bone making contact.

In addition to the highly efficient edge-of-hand blow, there are a few other open-handed blows which can be used for practical defense. None of these blows requires a high level of skill for effective application. These blows can be used in different ways to correspond to the situation; they can be used with moderate force when that would be suitable and they can be used with greater force against a vicious or dangerous assault.

**24.** The heel-of-palm blow can be delivered as a moderate, pushing action, or it can be delivered as a forceful, thrusting action. Curl your fingers back and strike with the fleshy part of the base of your palm.

**25.** The "Y" of your hand, between your extended fingers and thumb, can be used to hit at limited targets, close-in.

24

25

**26.** Poking blows, or distraction actions, can be applied with fingers together, as shown here . . .

**27.** . . . or with a claw-like thrust.

**28.** Using the heel of your palm, you can push up or thrust up under the nose . . .

**29.** . . . or you can use the pushing or thrusting action up under the chin.

**30.** The closed-finger stab can be delivered as a jabbing action into the muscle which is prominent at the side of the neck.

**31.** The claw-like poking blow can be used to distract by thrusting your hand *toward* the assailant's face, or it can be used as a blow which is completed by hitting his face with the palm of your hand, or, in the event of serious, dangerous assault, it can be used as a blow into the eyes. Hitting into the

26

27

eyes is a high-risk-of-injury blow. It is appropriate only if the assault is vicious and cannot be stopped with less risk of injury. Partners must be particularly careful in practice of this technique; slight contact involves possibility of eye injury. The distance shown in the photo is quite close enough for simulation practice.

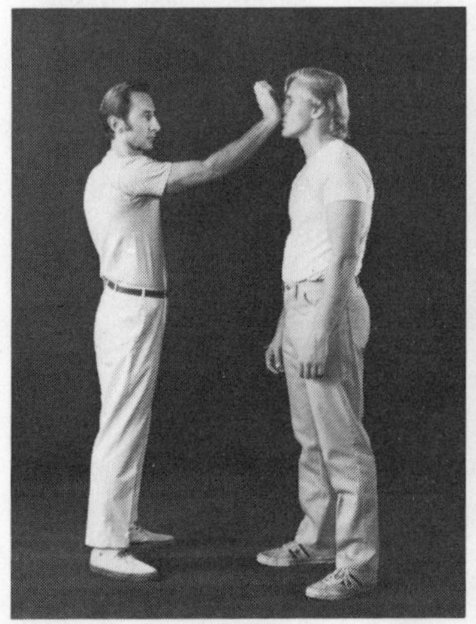

28

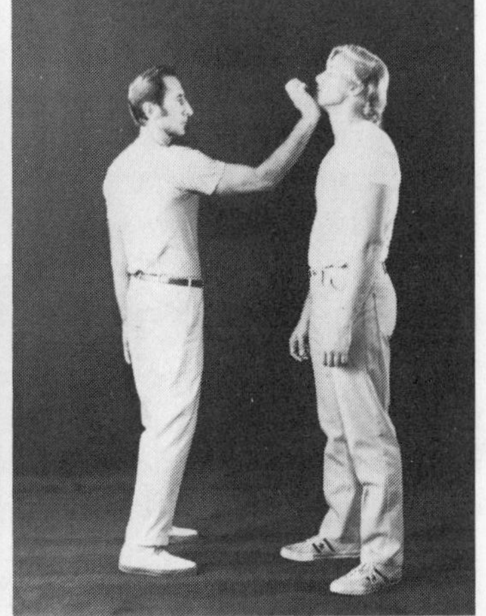

29

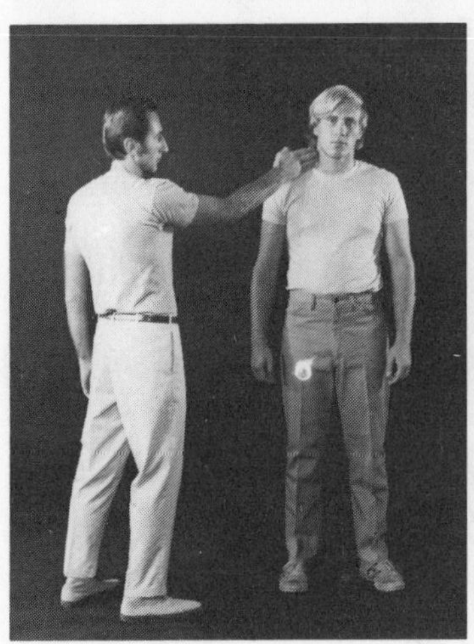

30

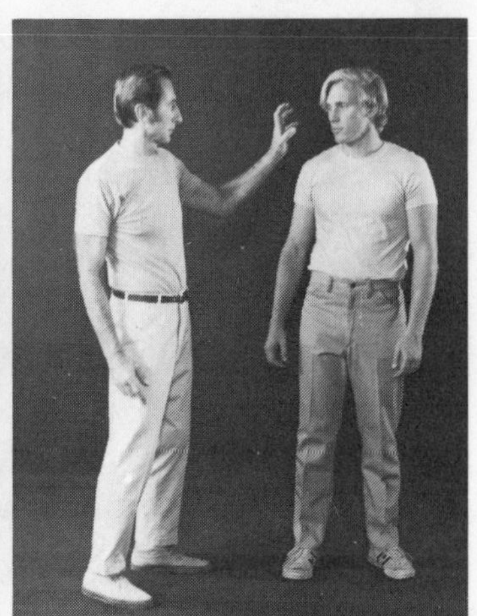

31

## FIST BLOWS

The effectiveness of a fist blow does not depend on the style of the blow, but on the amount of force delivered and on the body target. There are some fist blows which I recommend not because they deliver the greatest amount of force possible, but because they can be used effectively with moderate force.

If you already feel comfortable with and can use standard boxing fist blows, there is no need for you to change your style. You can add variety and versatility by incorporating additional hand blows which are useful for basic self-defense, but you need not discard boxing blows if you can use them with any degree of efficiency.

32. The karate-type fist blow is delivered with the two large knuckles. In traditional contest-oriented karate training, the fist blow is directed toward a target but no contact is made. Highly trained karate contestants can deliver perfectly controlled, full-power fist blows to within an inch or two of the opponent-partner's face. This requires considerable training and practice; the control and speed which are developed in practice can be maintained only with constant practice; without practice, it will be lost.

For practical self-defense, the objective is not the same as it is in contest karate; you need only develop the ability to deliver an effective blow without wasting energy; selection of the appropriate target is important and, as with all other techniques and tactics, the defense action must suit the situation.

33. Striking with the two large knuckles, an upward fist blow resembles the standard boxing upper-cut in its action.

34. The hammer blow is delivered with the edge of the fist and has limited, but useful application for basic self-defense.

35. An extended-knuckle blow has limited but useful application.

32

33

34

35

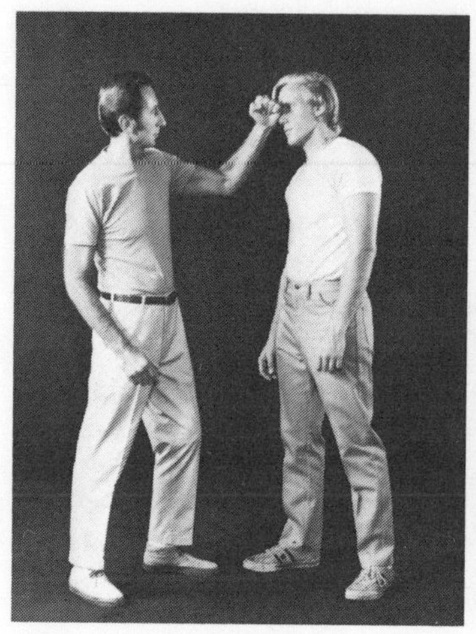

36

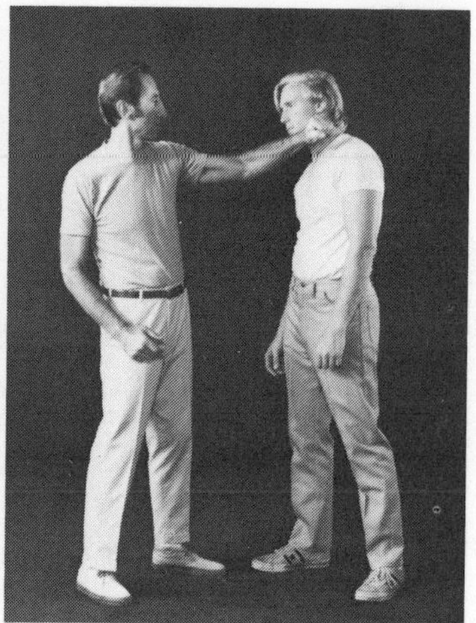

37

**36.** Striking down onto the bridge of the nose is a good technique for close-in defense.

**37.** Or, you can hit into the side of the neck with the hammer-like blow.

Selecting bony targets, the clavicle for instance, is more appropriate for movie fights than it is for real people. Hitting at a bony target has one of two effects—either nothing happens, or bones are broken. To break bones, a high degree of skill and force would be needed; since we define practical self-defense as protection with the least possible use of force, learning to break bones with hammer blows is an unsuitable procedure.

**38.** Using traditional boxing fist blows, or karate-style punching, select a target area which is more suitable for defense use than head or face blows. The mid-body can be struck without as much force as is needed to hit into bony, protected body target areas. You can strike straight in . . .

**39.** . . . or hit in an upward direction.

40. Against an annoying person, the extended knuckle can be used with a grinding action just below the last rib.

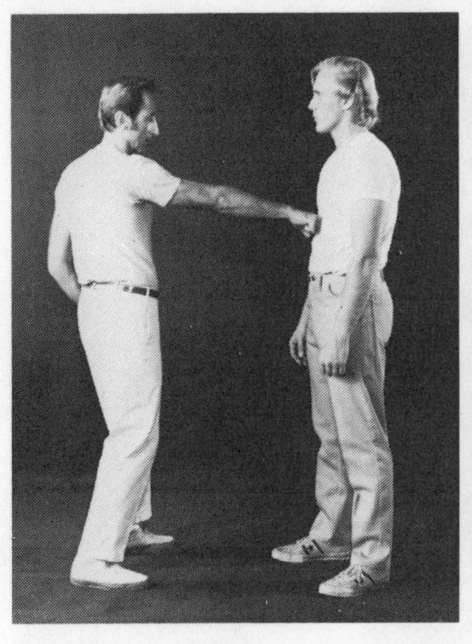

38

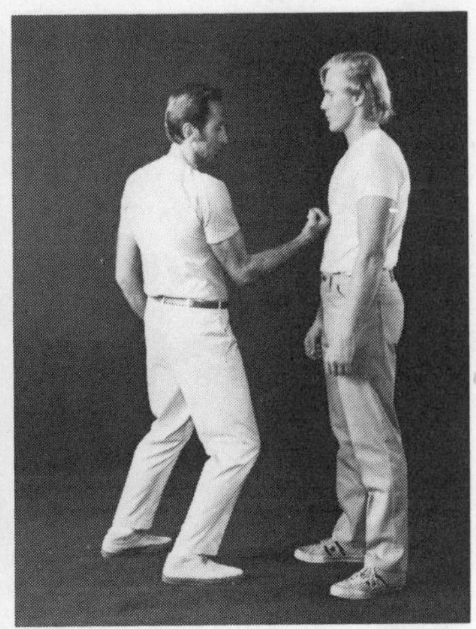

39

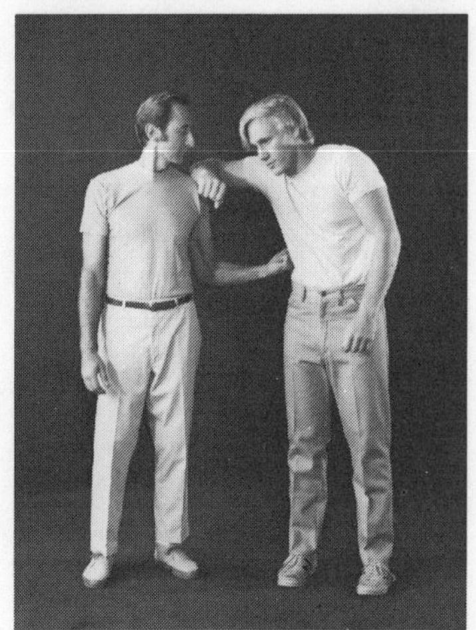

40

41. An effective elbow blow for practical self-defense is delivered straight back, or . . .

42. . . . in an upward direction, with a circular motion.

43. The target areas for striking with the elbow are into the mid-body, and . . .

44. . . . into the side of the head, neck or face.

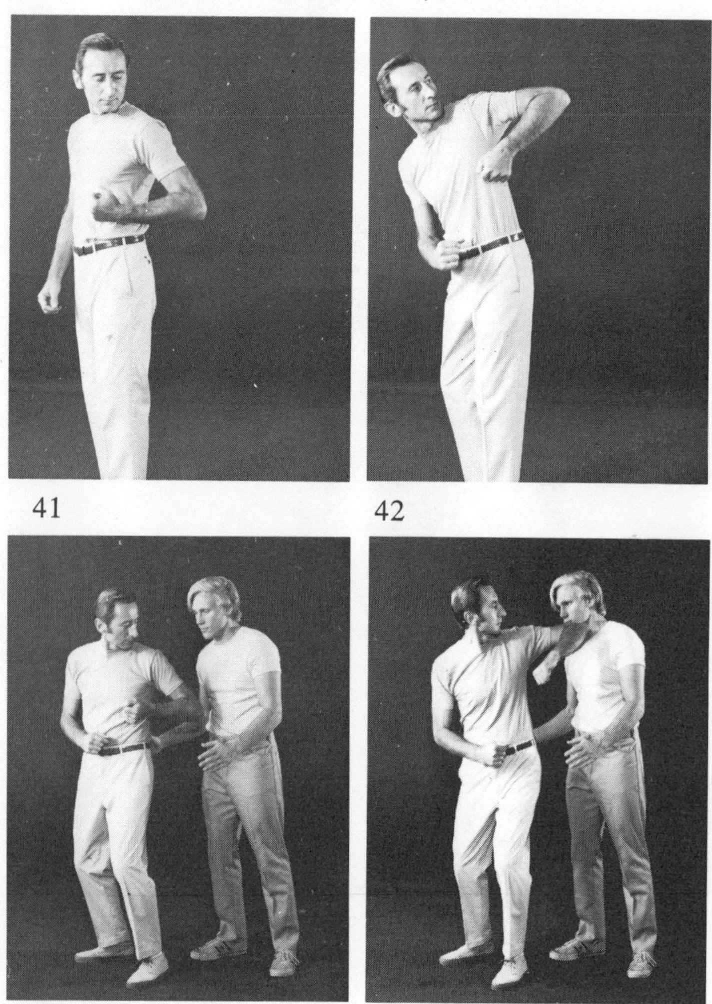

41 42

43 44

**KICKING FOR SELF-DEFENSE—FAIR?**

In the United States, there is a fairly general aversion to kicking; we think that bad guys kick, but that good guys do not. Street fighters kick, but their victims, by some odd kind of reasoning, are prohibited from kicking in self-defense because kicking is "dirty" fighting.

There is no "fair" assault. According to my definition, techniques, in themselves are neither fair nor unfair. The total situation, including techniques, has to be evaluated. Fist blows, which would be "fair" in one kind of situation, would be grossly unfair in another. If two individuals, of approximately the same size, weight and skill, enter willingly into a match and both use fist blows, fist blows are fair. If a strong heavy individual assaults a small frail person with fist blows, fist blows are unfair.

If two individuals enter into a match in which foot blows are forbidden, if one of them kicks, it is clearly unfair. Using kicks in self-defense against an assailant is neither fair nor unfair, since the concept of fair doesn't apply.

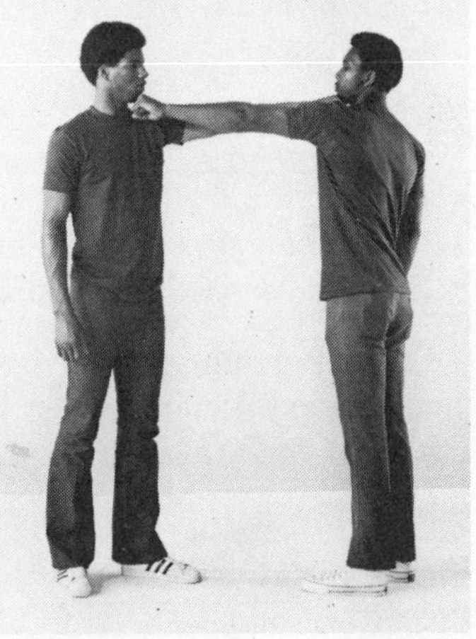

45

**45.** The men shown here are about equal in size, weight and fighting skill. If they were to engage in contest, they could use any group of techniques so long as they both followed the same set of rules. They could engage in a fair contest.

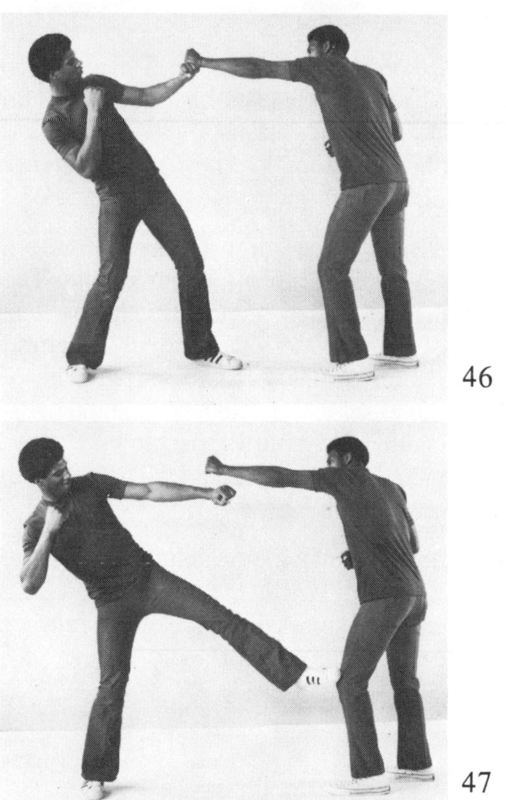

46

47

Now, imagine that the situation is different; the man on the right is threatening assault; the man on the left does not want to fight and makes his position clear.

If the belligerent person insists on fighting, the defense should be as efficient as possible and on terms which give the defending individual the best chance of stopping the assault without getting hurt.

**46.** Rather than moving in to use his hands, thereby putting himself within hitting range of his assailant, a more effective defense action is moving back out of range of his adversary's reach . . .

**47.** . . . ready to kick, if it is necessary.

**48.** It is even more clear, when we select mis-matched individuals, that the smaller person has no chance at all of exchanging fist blows with a larger, stronger assailant. If she tries to use hand blows in this kind of situation, she is making herself more vulnerable to his punch.

**49.** But, using kicks, she can stop the intended assault and make an orderly defense.

We must consciously avoid the assumptions of sport matches (and of combat) when preparing to cope with the possibility of assault. We choose the most effective defense actions possible; we use the least force possible; if foot blows are appropriate, we use them.

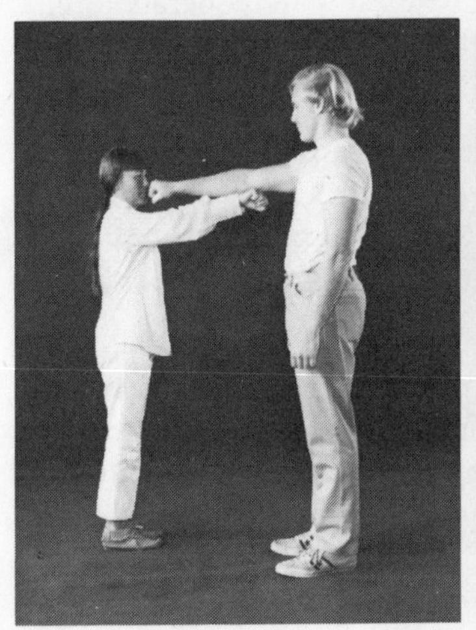

48

49

## HOW TO KICK

The spectacular high kicks taught in traditional karate and savate have no practical application for self-defense. The high, difficult kicks are for contest. In tournament, points are given for high kicks, only. The high kicks and the leaping kicks can be learned only with considerable effort and continuing practice. When practice of the high kicks is discontinued, skill diminishes. Moreover, those individuals who have the greatest need for self-defense are those least likely to be able to learn and use high kicks.

The kicks which I have adapted for self-defense are modified versions of karate and savate kicking. They are aimed at low body targets and they can be learned by most people with relative ease. These kicks can be used with moderate force, when appropriate, and with considerable power when necessary.

The practical kicks for self-defense can be applied from a standstill, and from a moving-about circumstance. Practical kicks can be delivered regardless of the type of footwear; you do not have to change into or out of your ordinary shoes to use basic kicks.

In addition to keeping you out of fist range of your assailant, kicks offer other advantages. Your leg is stronger than your arm, so you can deliver a more powerful blow with your foot than with your hand. Though street fighters use kicks, they do not expect their intended victims to kick. You have, therefore, the element of surprise in your favor when you kick for defense.

### Snap Kick

50. Very close in, a kick can be delivered with the inside edge of your shoe or foot. The action is snappy; you recover immediately to avoid loss of balance.

51. The outside edge of your foot, or shoe, can deliver a snappy kick of moderate or considerable force, depending on the circumstance. The entire length of the edge of your shoe is the striking area; this positioning ensures that you can hit the target without having to practice for precise accuracy.

50 51

52 53

**Stamp Kick**

52. Using the bottom of your foot or shoe, you can deliver a stamping kick forward . . .

53. . . . or to the rear.

54

54. The edge-of-shoe snap-kick can be delivered to the rear, with relatively little practice to develop proficiency.

**KICKING TARGETS**

55. When you practice with your partner, you must always observe the safety rules. After you learn the correct gesture and delivery of the kicks in solo practice, you may practice with your partner *without* making contact. Some photos illustrate how the kicks would be applied in defense use, but for practice, you need not get any closer than shown here. You can simulate the kicks with realistic vigor if you are careful to avoid contact.

56. The target for the inside-edge-of-shoe kick is low on the shin; this is the only efficient application of this kick.

57. The outside-edge-of-shoe snap kick can be delivered low on the shin, or into the mid-shin. You do not need to be

perfectly accurate; anywhere along the shin, from just below the knee down to the ankle, is a suitable target. You can kick into the ankle, as well. The edge-of-shoe snap kick is delivered fairly close in for practical defense. Highly trained individuals can apply edge-of-foot snap kicks with the leg fully extended, but this requires practice and training.

55

56

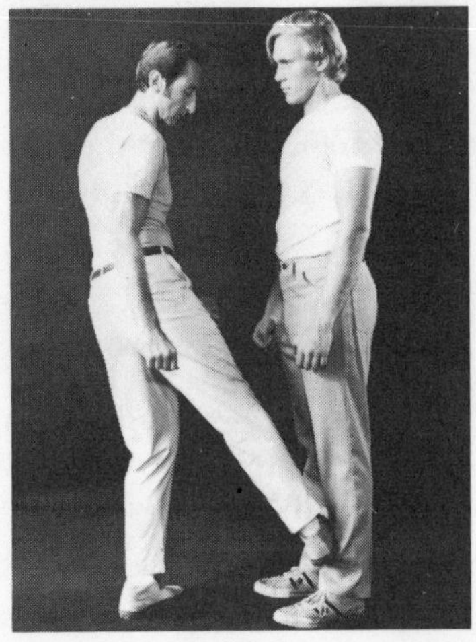

57

58

59

58. The target for the stamping-out kick is the knee. There is considerable latitude in the angle of kick; you can kick directly into the front of the knee, somewhat to the side of the kneecap; into the side of the leg at the knee, and . . .

59. . . . into the back of the knee if you position yourself for it.

All kicks delivered to this target are useful, but the most effective is delivered at about a 45-degree angle, half-way between the front and the side of the knee-cap. This angle is most likely to put him off balance and a vigorous kick could put him on the ground.

You can use kicks from almost any position, or angle of relationship to your assailant.

60. To the rear, you can use the edge-of-shoe snap kick effectively without having to turn around or shift your foot position. You can kick back into the shin . . .

61. . . . and follow through with a scraping action down the shin to finish with a stamping kick down onto the instep. Or, you could use the stamp onto the instep as a separate action.

62. You can kick back using the stamping kick into the knee.

Without making contact on your partner, practice delivering all the kicks from different angles and be sure to alternate right and left foot kicks to avoid dependence on your strong side.

60

61

62

63

64

## Hooking Kick

The circle kick, or hooking kick of sport karate, can be modified for self-defense application by selecting a more practical target. The rules of sport karate require that kicks be directed above the belt or they are not valid for contest points. The ability to use high kicks is developed only with considerable practice and training and is maintained only through constant practice.

Kicking at the knee, or into the thigh, converts the hooking kick into a technique which can be used for self-defense.

**63.** Pivot on your non-kicking foot so that you can bear body weight without losing your balance; draw your kicking leg up . . .

**64.** . . . and kick in a circular, hooking manner.

Be careful not to make contact on your partner. The kick should be snappy; hit with the toe of your shoe. Practice this kick on left and right sides.

## BLOCK & PARRY

Self-defense is more defensive when it *prevents* blows than when it involves *exchange* of blows. A great many assaultive actions begin with a reaching or punching action. Instead of permitting that action to be completed, avoid it, deflect it or block it.

Blocks and parries are methods of avoiding getting hit; they are similar actions with overlapping function. A block action implies that force is being countered with force, whereas parrying implies deflection of the oncoming blow. For practical self-defense the difference is not critical and I tend to use the words interchangeably.

### Slapping Parry

65. Begin in fairly slow motion. The partner who plays the role of assailant reaches out, first with one hand and then the other. As he reaches out with his right hand, slap/parry cross-body with your open palm to divert and deflect the blow. It should be a snappy, vigorous action and not a pushing action. As he reaches out with his left hand, slap the outside of his arm cross-body with your right hand. Practice the cross-body slap/parry until you are fairly comfortable doing it. The cross-body parry at the outside of his arm has the virtue of putting your assailant into awkward position.

65

66

67

66. Practice also, hitting at the inside of his arm. This technique is not generally as efficient as the parry which moves his arm across his body, but it is a useful alternative. Practice against his right-handed reach and against his left-handed reach.

#### Slashing Parry

67. You can use open-handed slashing blows to parry high blows, as shown, or you can use them to parry low blows. Practice using the slash/parry against reaching or simulated punching high and low and against right and left blows.

68. You can use double-handed slashing parries if you are out to the side of the reaching arm. This is an excellent tactic, though somewhat limited in application.

#### Fist & Forearm Blocks & Parries

69. The edge-of-fist parry is an effective technique, but requires somewhat greater precision than does the open-handed parry. If you feel comfortable using this technique, practice it in a manner which will allow for a margin of error. This photo shows a precision block . . .

68

69

70

71

**70.** . . . but if you aim for your target so that your forearm blocks if you fail to make direct contact with your fist, you have greater flexibility.

**71.** If you block with your forearm, you must be closer in to your assailant than if you use the open-handed slash.

72

73

The forearm block is strong and requires less accuracy than a hand block or parry. Practice all variations of the forearm block, remembering that if you move his hitting arm across his body, it is the most effective way of deflecting his intended action. Practice upward forearm blocks with your right and your left arm: Practice cross-body blocks with right and left arm.

**72.** You can practice the forearm block with your hand fisted, as shown in the previous photos, or with your hand open, as in this photo.

**73.** If you are at the outside of the assailant's arm, you can use a double-forearm block.

**BLOCKING THE FOUR QUARTERS**

This is a practice procedure to develop appropriate response to a reaching or punching arm.

Partners begin practice in very slow motion. You should experience success and block correctly; this is the foundation for improvement of skill.

When you have practiced slowly for as long as it takes you to feel comfortable blocking high or low blows, right or left blows, then practice to develop greater speed and practice the various blocking techniques.

74. Partners stand just out of fist hitting range. At first, partner simulating the assailant should repeat a simple sequence of two high blows, right . . .

75. . . . and left, followed by . . .

76. . . . two low blows, right and . . .

77. . . . left.

74

75

76

77

Practice this simple procedure a few times, then without accelerating the speed of delivery, assailant partner begins to mix his blows so that they do not follow any pattern. As partners develop the skill to respond quickly and appropriately, the practice procedure can become more and more complex and include feints and faking actions.

When partners are fairly well able to block to the appropriate quarter, you may choose a final mode of practice which is fairly realistic without danger of hurting each other. The assailant-playing partner attempts to slap or touch the defending partner on the upper arm or chest, using only the palm of either hand, or he attempts to grip either wrist. If you follow these rules carefully, it is possible to practice as though defending against realistic assault.

If you can use the parry/block actions with moderate skill, you can handle a great many kinds of assault with the least possible use of force or strength.

## TRAINING AIDS

Because the defense actions must be simulated for safety in practice, it is helpful to improvise training aids which can be used for hitting and kicking. They can be improvised from inexpensive materials and used almost anywhere.

### Hand Blows

To practice fully-released hand blows, hitting as hard as you can, place several layers of towel on a solid, table-height surface. Hit with moderate force, using the edge-of-hand chop, until you are certain that you are striking correctly. Increase the force of your hand blows until you are delivering full power blows. This practice is simply to allow you to experience the feeling of hitting as hard as you can. If you hit correctly, you should be able to hit as hard as you can without hurting your hand.

78

79

**78.** Improvise a hitting stick by padding a length of dowel with foam rubber (poly foam/plastic foam) or toweling. Fasten the padding with tape—do not use pins, clamps or metal fasteners. Partners take turns holding the stick, as shown, so that each can practice hitting an arm-like object.

**79.** Practice left and right blows; practice blocking and slashing. Partners should move the stick in such a way that it simulates reaching and punching arm movements.

**Swinging Ball**

Fasten a small rubber ball to the end of a length of rope. You can improvise this training aid by putting the rubber ball into a sock and tying the sock to the cord, or rope.

80. Partners take turns holding the rope so that the ball is at approximately knee level, as shown, where it is used to practice kicking for precision. Hitting this small, swinging object is more difficult than kicking at a leg target. Do not kick with force; the object of the practice is to kick at a moving target.

To practice hand blows against the swinging ball target, partners take turns holding it at about chest height. Hit the ball lightly. Practice right hand and left hand blows. Practice the various hand blows.

**Kicking Against the Padded Stick**

81. Partners can take turns moving the padded stick to simulate a moving leg. Kicking the stick does not require as much precision as kicking the swinging ball, but more precision than kicking the bag. Kicking the stick cannot be done with as much power as kicking the bag, but you can kick the stick harder than you can kick the swinging ball. This practice combines moderate force and precision. Alternate left and right kicks.

**Power Kicking**

82. You can improvise a kicking target by filling a laundry or duffel bag with crushed paper. Partners take turns holding it in place, as shown. If you want a heavier bag, add sand, making a mix of crushed paper and sand to suit your individual need. Practice right and left kicks. Practice the edge-of-shoe snap kick.

80

81

82

83

**83.** Practice the stamping kick.

Practice kicks to the rear.

You can place the hitting bag onto a solid table-height surface and practice hand blows of all types.

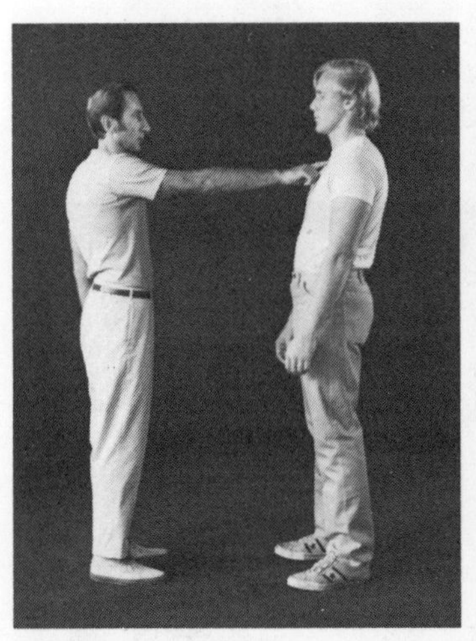

84

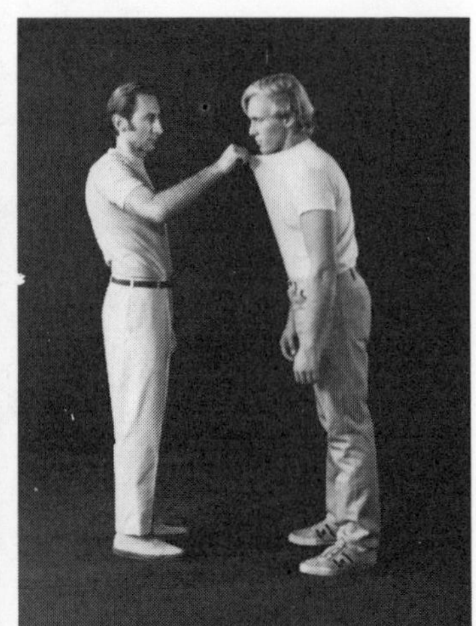

85

**STRONG & WEAK LINES: The Going-With Principle**

Using strength to oppose strength is not an efficient way to deal with assault. To counter a power blow with greater power takes practice, training, muscle-development and, finally, it still leaves the advantage with the stronger person. A ninety-nine-pound weakling who lifts weights, works out and builds himself up to his maximum strength is somewhat better off than when he was at his minimum level of strength. Nevertheless, if he tried to match his strength against the strength of a 200-pound assailant, he would have a considerable handicap.

A more reasonable concept than power-against-power is that of working against the weak line. The concept of working against weakness, sometimes called the "going-with" principle, can be applied in a number of ways. If your adversary shoves, you do not shove back, but you use his action to assist your defense action. If you are gripped, you do not attempt to wrench yourself free with force, but you work against the weak part of the grip.

Working against the weak line, rather than opposing strength with strength, gives an added element of surprise to your defense actions; it is the unexpected response. If someone pushes you, he expects you to pull back; if someone shoves you, he expects you to shove him in return.

The use of weak-line actions for self-defense will be applied in a number of the defenses you will practice. When you are cautioned not to work against the strong line, but to apply the technique against the weak line, it is a way of reminding you that an efficient defense is one which uses the least amount of strength or power for effective result.

Experiment with your partner to demonstrate to each other how easy it is to work against the weak line in comparison with struggling against the strong line.

84. If your partner stands in a normal stance, as shown, you can push him off balance with fingertip pressure.

85. Or you can pull him forward, off balance, with two fingers.

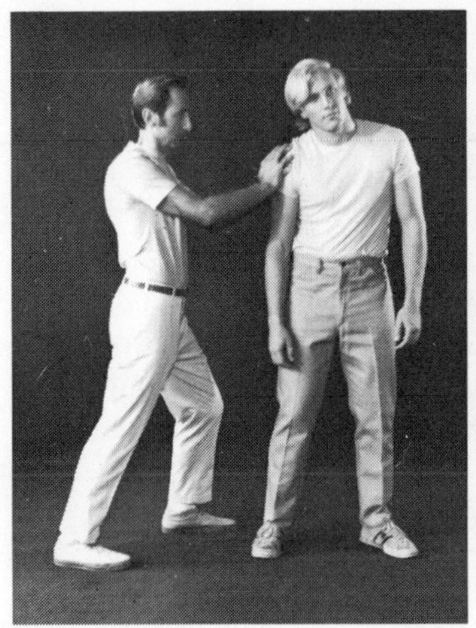

86

87

**86.** He will not be vulnerable to a push from the side if he is in a normal stance, though he would still be vulnerable to a push or pull from the front or back.

**87.** If, on the other hand, your partner places himself in a strong stance, the standard boxer's stance, as shown, or the ''T'' stance of the fencer, he cannot be opposed unless you know which is the weak line and which the strong line. If you try to oppose him against the strong line, considerable effort and power would be required.

**88.** If you work against his weak line, you can move him with relative ease. One-point balance is a weak, vulnerable stance. If your partner stands on one foot, you can push or pull him in any direction with very little effort.

88

# PART TWO

## FIGHTING STANCES? Pro & Con and an Alternative

The fighting stances of karate have become almost as well known as the flying kicks and board-breaking tricks and they have almost as little application for practical self-defense.

In contest, a fighting stance makes sense; in training, many of the formal routines begin and end with a fighting stance; in the movies, the karate fighter usually takes a fighting stance before he goes into his act.

Fighting stances, as a part of self-defense in the real world, are of dubious psychological value much of the time, and of limited tactical value.

A fighting stance has the greatest value in a sport match. In tournament, the whole point is to engage in a "fight" in which both contestants are willing participants. The situation in self-defense is quite different. A prudent person avoids fighting; a prudent person avoids the appearance of being willing to fight if there is any possibility of handling the situation without resorting to physical action.

There are some times when a fighting stance is useful for handling threat of assault, but other times when a fighting stance is neither appropriate nor desirable and might have negative value. Against a back attack, a body grab, a mugging or choking assault, it is impossible to take a fighting stance. It would be absurd to take a fighting stance in preparation for dealing with merely annoying, hostile behavior.

Responding to the threat of assault by taking a fighting stance tells your adversary that he is calling the shots. We are accustomed to thinking that the only positive answer to "I am going to hit you," is the reply: "If you do, I am going to hit back." There is still another choice, a positive alternative, which is; "No, you are not going to hit me!" This refusal to accept his terms, without a show of counter-hostility, shows that you have not lost control of yourself or of the situation. If you take a fighting stance, you relinquish the choice of positive, non-aggressive control; you are committed to fighting if your adversary feels challenged by your stance.

The first choice response to the threat of assault is to avoid the role of passive victim, to avoid the role of counter-aggressor, but to take on the attitude and behavior of self-assertion.

Cowering down or showing fright is the passive role. Taking a fighting stance is an aggressive role. Taking a ready stance is assertive action.

## READY STANCES

If there is any possibility of avoiding the use of force, you can take a ready stance, which is neutral in gesture, permits you to negotiate, and allows you to move quickly and defensively if you must. Taking a ready stance is like putting up an invisible guard; you have flexibility of response, you are prepared to block, you can kick, etc., yet nothing about the way you are standing or holding your hands indicates belligerence.

**89.** The natural-looking, thoughtful guard assumed by the right man does not suggest aggression or challenge. Realizing that a threat is developing, he takes a modified boxer's foot stance for strong balance, puts one hand up to his face and places the other hand under his arm.

**90.** From the ready position, he can move quickly, using a hand blow, or simply thrusting his hand toward the adversary to startle and disconcert him.

**91.** Or, if the situation warrants it, he can quickly hit and kick.

92. Another ready stance is taken with both hands held in front of you. Your right hand is fisted and covered by your open left hand. Create a tension by pushing forward with your right hand as you pull back with your left. If necessary, you can move quickly, using a hand blow, or you can hit and kick from this position.

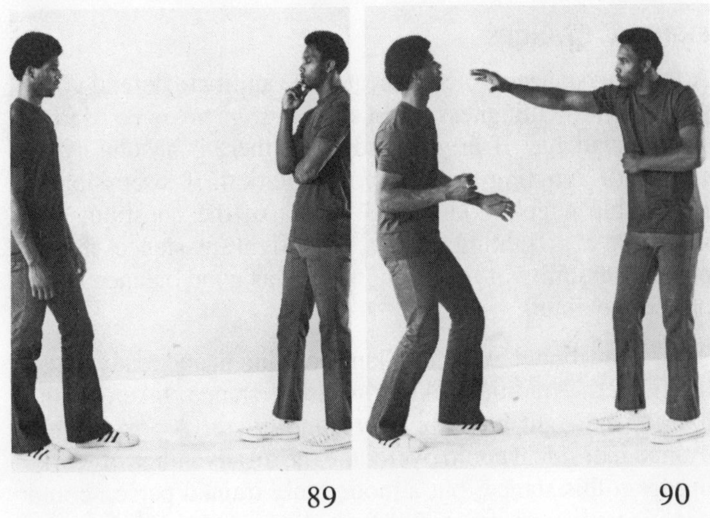

89 90

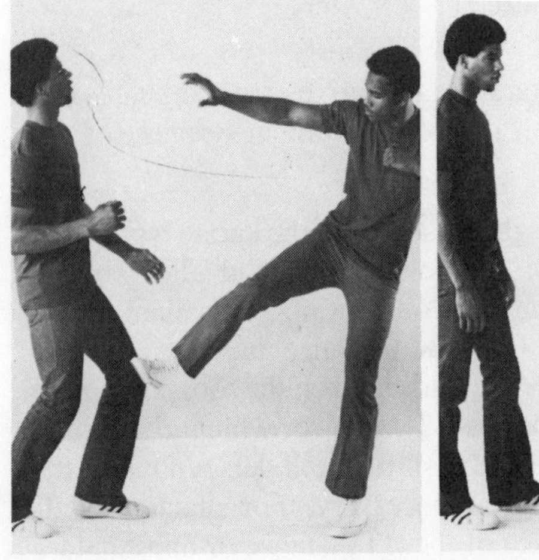

91

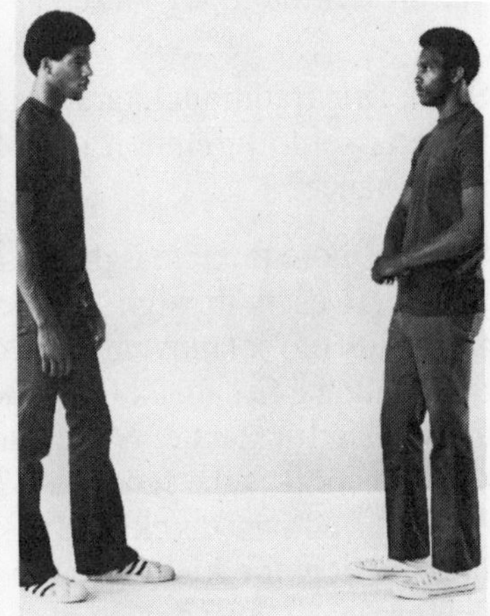

92

93. Another ready position which is a casual, non-aggressive posture, is the folded-arm stance. Your hands are fisted, or open. Instead of pulling both arms into your body, which would inhibit movement, create a tension by pulling back with one arm as you push forward with the other. You can move quickly, if necessary.

## FIGHTING STANCES

A fighting stance, which indicates the ability to defend yourself and the willingness to do so, can *sometimes* be used to good advantage. If in your judgment there is absolutely no chance of avoiding physical confrontation, if discussion or reasonable negotiation would be out of the question, you might take a fighting stance. The fighting stance should permit flexibility of response, as well as good balance and a protective guard.

94. Confronted by an assailant, moving in and ready to use his fists, the traditional kung fu horse stance, taken by the man at the right is simply *not* appropriate. A very highly trained individual could overcome the disadvantage of working from this stance, but a moderately trained person could not. There is no protective guard, the foot position does not permit flexible body shifts.

95. This traditional karate stance gives a good guard, but there is some limitation of foot movement because of the wide stance.

96. A more flexible fighting stance of the karate type is one which gives both high and low guards and allows more flexibility of foot movement. Confronting an assailant who is threatening a fist attack, this karate stance might be useful as a disconcerting tactic. Note, particularly, the foot position of this stance. It is the fencer's "T" stance, which gives good balance, allows quick body shifts, and lets you use the forward leg for kicking, if necessary. For practical self-defense, take your choice of the "T" stance or the standard boxing stance foot position; both are efficient.

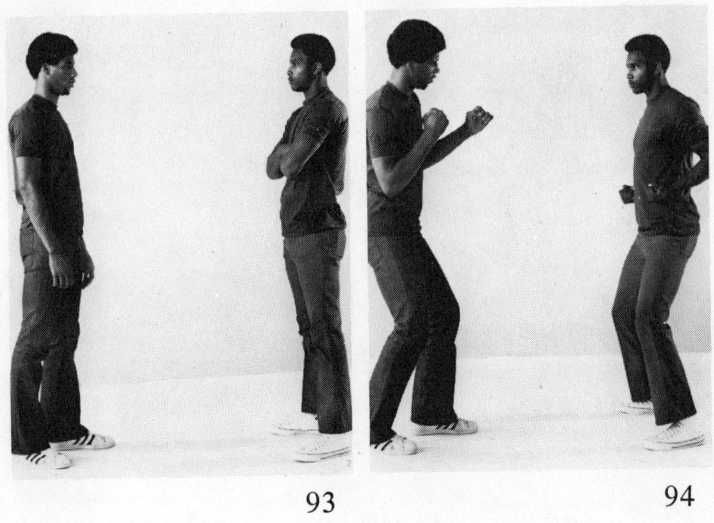

93 94

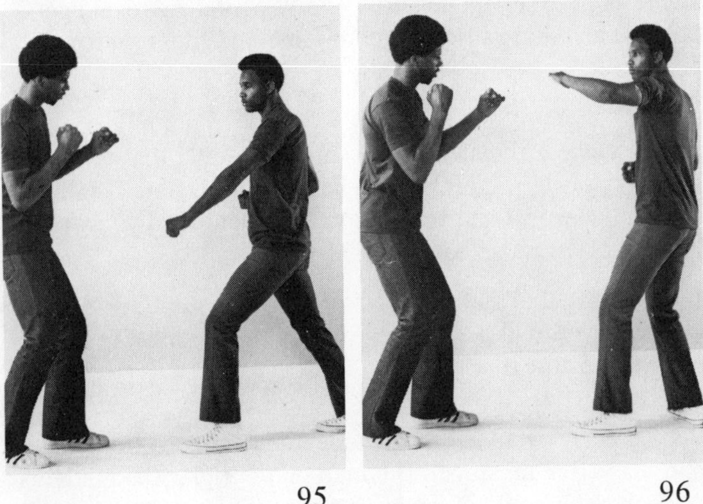

95 96

97

97. Taking a standard boxing fighting stance has a very special advantage, for it gives the appearance of conventionality. From this stance, it appears that you will use the same style of action as he intends to use against you, adding the element of surprise to your defense. The boxing fighting stance is an excellent posture—it gives good guard and good balance and allows flexibility of hand and foot movement.

## GESTURES OF ASSERTION

To convince a threatening, hostile individual that you will not be a passive victim, your behavior must be totally believable. Your words and your body movements and your facial expression must be compatible.

If you have not had enough practice in standing up for yourself, you will need to rehearse the appropriate response to physical threat.

98. The left man in this photo is threatening by his gesture and his verbal message. The man on the right, though he is not cowering down in fright, is too neutral in his stance. He appears vulnerable.

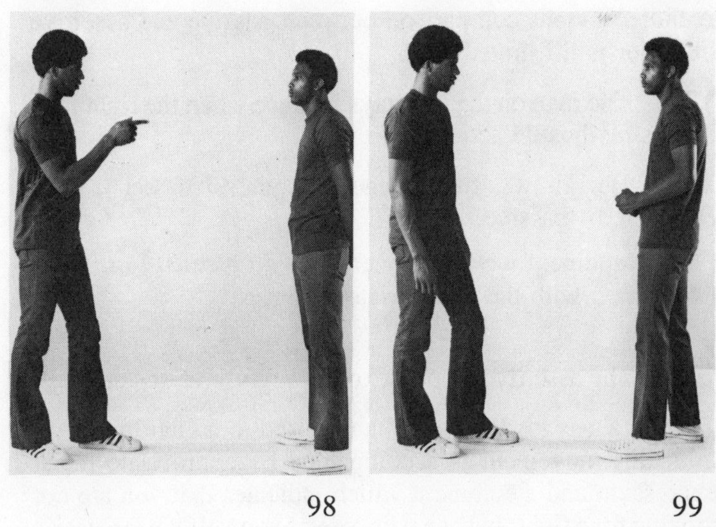

98 99

99. In this photo, the slight shift of body weight and the placement of his hands have made the man on the right appear more assertive. He is well-balanced, his hands are ready to use, but he is not displaying counter-aggression. His verbal and physical message is clear; "I can take care of myself, if I have to." He makes direct eye contact.

Partners should take turns playing the part of threatening and being threatened. Whether or not you feel comfortable doing this, it is essential preparation for being assertive. In fact, if you feel extremely uncomfortable when you behave assertively, it probably means that you need this role-playing practice and can benefit from it. Partners can help each other by being very serious about this procedure. The threatening partner should make his threat believable by body gesture, tone of voice and facial expression. The partner who is rehearsing the assertive role must respond in a convincing manner; his body gesture, tone of voice and facial expression should convey the message: Don't touch me!

You will both know when you are doing this properly; the difference between non-assertive and assertive behavior can sometimes be quite subtle.

A more obvious comparison between passive and assertive behavior is illustrated here.

**100.** The man on the left stays in place when the right man begins his hostile action.

**101.** He allows the intended aggressive act to be completed—passive behavior.

For the moment we are concerned with assertive *attitudes* rather than with the appropriate defenses.

**102.** The assertive response to the aggressive gesture . . .

**103.** . . . is to step back, hand raised in a guarding position; this movement is accompanied by appropriate facial expression and a comment which indicates that you are not looking for a fight, but can take care of yourself if necessary.

Don't mumble your words; speak clearly. Don't shout; speak loud enough to be heard. Don't smile; maintain a serious facial expression. Maintain eye contact.

Partners can critique each other. Practice this procedure until you feel quite comfortable in the rehearsal of assertive response to threat of assault. This is an essential part of preventive self-defense.

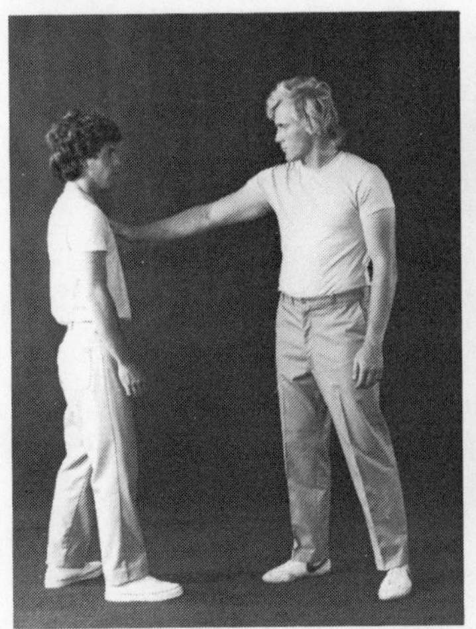

100

101

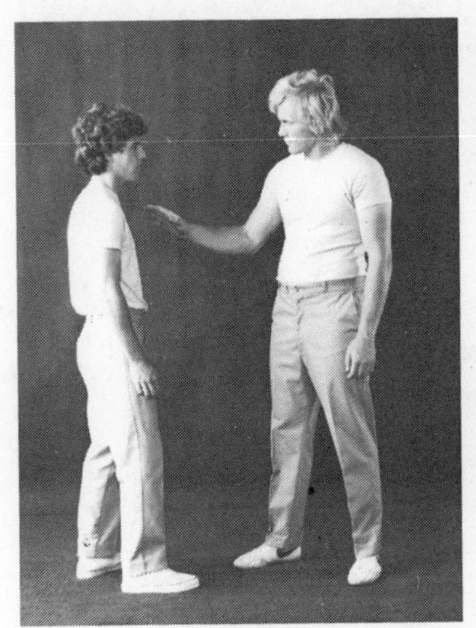

102

103

**RESPONSE TO FRONT REACH**

A high percentage of hostile or aggressive actions begin with a reaching arm. You do not have to wait until the aggressive action is completed; stop the arm before it touches you. You do not have to think about the specific intention; your response would be the same if the adversary were trying to grab, poke, pull, shove or slap. Your response is to the reaching arm, not to a specific, completed action.

As a practice procedure, take turns stopping the reaching arm with the various parries and blocking techniques.

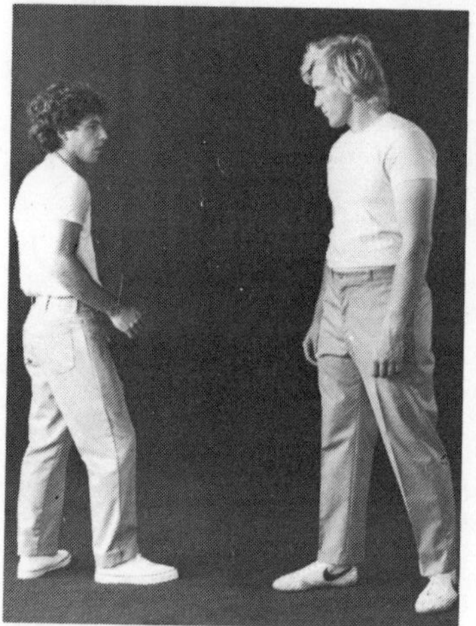

104

105

**104.** Partners stand within normal distance, as though talking.

**105.** When the assailant partner starts to reach out, defending partner steps back and parries.

Practice parrying and blocking right- and left-handed reaches. Practice stopping low reaching gestures, as though the intent were to grip your wrist. Stop reaches simulating intended cloth grab at your chest. Stop head-height reaches which simulate a gesture toward your face.

Though you need know only two or three of the parry/block actions for basic self-defense, practice all of them so that you can select the ones which are most comfortable for you. The parry actions are fundamental to efficient defense, even though they are not flashy or spectacular.

Parrying is assertive, rather than counter-aggressive. Parrying stops the intended aggressive action, and it conveys the message that you are capable of defending yourself. It is a way of taking control, using the least possible degree of force.

**QUICK RESPONSE TO BACK THREAT**

If you can also respond to threat of assault from the rear *before* the assault has been completed, you can cope much more efficiently with such attempts. You should, of course, be able to deal with completed assaults, but responding before the intended action is completed is easier and you are less vulnerable if you respond sooner.

Take turns playing the role of assailant and defending partner. There are various cues to which you respond: a light touch, a sight cue, even subtle sound cues should make you alert. Obviously, you do not respond to such cues as "danger" unless the situation suggests the possibility of danger.

Practice procedures: Standing behind you, your partner touches you lightly on the shoulder. Turn quickly with one arm in a blocking position. Take turns doing this until you respond without hesitation.

Standing behind you, your partner moves his hand until you can see it out of the corner of your eye. The moment you see movement, turn around with one arm in blocking position. Take turns doing this.

If you are practicing in a quiet area, you can take turns giving each other sound cues.

You are rehearsing the prudent response to the clues which signal "danger behind you." You are safer if you turn to face a possible threat than if you keep your back turned to it.

When you have practiced the turn-and-block gesture, proceed to practice responding to assault attempts such as grabbing or choking from behind. Instead of giving a slight cue, partners will now take turns attempting to complete a particular action. Use a variety of parry and block actions as you practice.

**106.** For example, your partner starts the action of a finger choke. Do not allow him to complete his intended action.

**107.** The instant you feel his hands touch you, wheel around sharply and block/slash his arm . . .

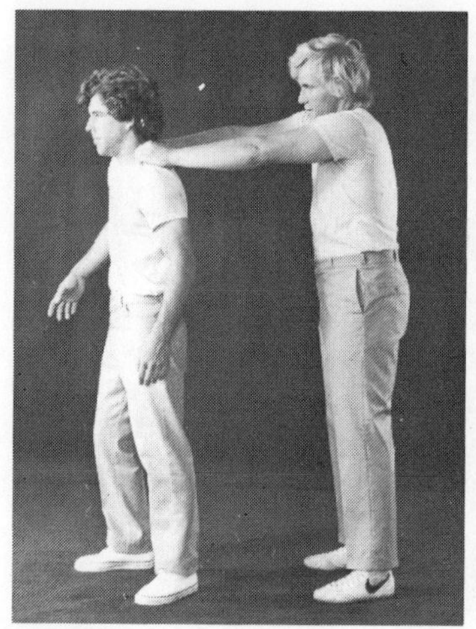

106

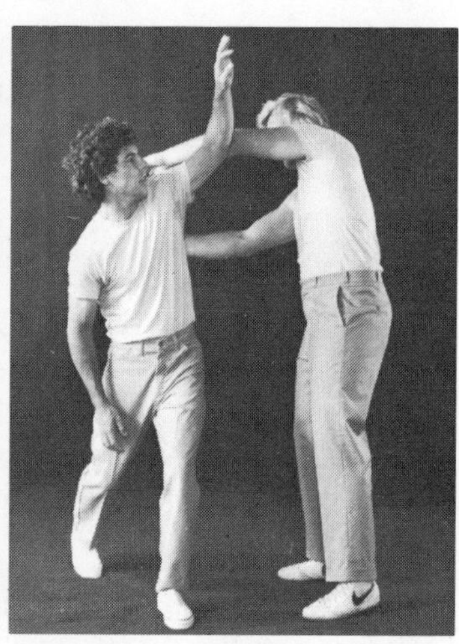

107

108. . . . kick into the shin. Complete the defense with appropriate hand and foot blows.

108

**DISTRACTION**

Against a serious assault, distraction is a way of gaining a time-and-attention advantage over your assailant. Distraction can be thrusting hand movements, yelling, throwing an object toward the assailant's face or rapid foot movement.

Except in the instance where you would *not* want to startle your assailant, such as close-in knife threat, loud yelling, rapid movements or a thrown object will disconcert, disorient, and confuse him. Even when the thrown object cannot hurt him, it is distracting.

Distraction can divert an intended assault and give you time to move out of range; it can give you a few seconds of time in which to put yourself in good guard, ready to hit and kick.

Whenever an intended victim behaves in an unexpected manner, it disrupts the planned action of the assailant.

109

110

111

112

### Feinting Distractions

Feinting actions are excellent tactical moves for self-defense. Feinting is a diversion; the assailant reacts to your feint or fake, giving you a chance to start your planned defense.

**109.** A quick thrusting hand movement toward his face makes him draw back . . .

**110.** . . . and you complete your defense with kicks or other appropriate actions.

**111.** A sudden arm movement upward, can get his attention for an instant . . .

**112.** . . . and allow you to kick, or hit as appropriate.

**113.** If you feint low, faking a kick, for instance . . .

**114.** . . . he will react to your feinting action . . .

113

114

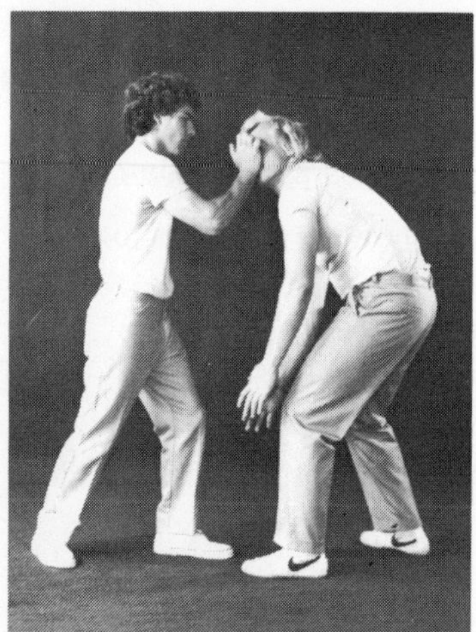

115

**115.** . . . allowing you to use hand blows, high.

In general, the best use of feinting actions is to the opposite area to which you plan your serious defense. If you feint with your left hand, you can hit with your right. If you fake a high blow, you can kick; if you kick low, you can use hand blows.

When you practice with your partner, you do not have the advantage of surprise which you would have in actual defense. But you will find that even when he knows you are going to use a feinting action, he will still have a slight reaction. Use your imagination as you practice; remember that an unexpected action draws a reaction.

### SIDE-STEP & KICK

Any tactic which is unexpected and which takes you out of fist range of the assailant gives you an advantage. The combination of evading his intended assault and hitting him has a two-fold effect: You are, in fact, letting him move first, but instead of allowing yourself to be hit, you hit him first. If there is any question about who is the aggressor, this tactic makes it clear that he is initiating the first hostile move. Though you hit first, it is in response to his aggression. You are clearly defending yourself, not starting a fight.

**116.** Whenever possible, keep some distance between yourself and a threatening individual; allow space in which to maneuver. Defending partner is on the right.

**117.** As he moves forward to attack, take a deep step to the outside of his moving arm . . .

116

117

118

**118.** . . . and without hesitation, kick into the side of his knee. If you kick with vigor, you could put him on the ground.

**LEAP BACK & KICK**

A tactic similar to the side-step-and-kick tactic is the leap, or step back, followed by a kick. Practice leaping back, but if you are uncomfortable trying to leap, practice a modified version by taking a very long step back. The situation is similar to that described in the side-step-and-kick tactic.

**119.** Try, whenever possible, to allow space in which to maneuver if you are threatened.

**120.** As he makes his move, leap . . .

**121.** . . . or step back, out of range of his fist . . .

119 120

121

122

122. . . . and without hesitation, kick into his knee.

Continue with appropriate actions to complete your defense.

**SAFETY FALLING**

The falling techniques of judo are sometimes taught to students learning self-defense, but in my view, they are optional.

Those individuals who are interested in achieving functional skill and who follow the safety rules carefully, will not be thrown, nor will they throw their practice partner.

If you are interested in gaining more than basic skill in self-defense, then you might wish to learn the proper manner of falling safely.

There is another advantage to learning how to fall correctly; if you stumble or are pushed, you can fall onto a hard surface with less likelihood of injury.

The fundamental actions of safety falling are curling and rolling. Judo players, wrestlers and stunt men all use the same principle but with different stylistic actions. For self-defense, you need not be as skilled in falling as a judo player, wrestler or stunt man.

The curl-and-roll principle minimizes jarring shock to vulnerable parts of the body and allows the impact of a fall to be spread over the greatest possible surface, diminishing the shock of impact.

Curling is a way of reducing the distance you fall; if you resist the fall by stiffening your body, you fall more heavily and further. If you bend your knees and lower your body as you go down, you fall with less force.

**Back Fall**

**123.** When falling back, avoid hitting your head.

123

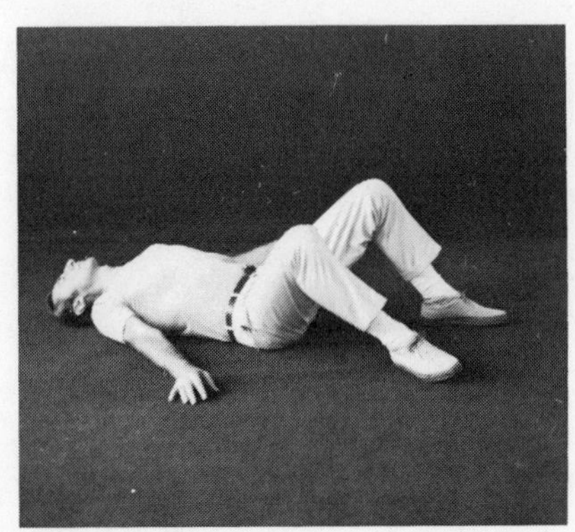

Avoid this.

124. The safe way of falling back, the curl-and-roll method, is: Bend your knees as you start to fall . . .

125. . . . curling your back to prepare for the rolling action . . .

126. . . . and tuck your head forward as you lower your body, and roll back easily (do not thrust yourself back) raising your legs and slapping the floor to absorb impact. Your arms are fully extended when you slap.

The slapping action is essential; if you time the slapping action to occur at the same moment as your upper back touches the floor, it will reduce the shock of impact. Do not bend your arms as you slap. Study the ending position in the photo again, after you have practiced a few times, to make certain that you are ending correctly.

124

125

126

**Side Fall**

127. An almost automatic reaction to being pushed, stumbling or falling, is to extend an arm to catch yourself. Although this response could prevent head injury, it is not a good way to fall.

128. If you fall onto your extended arm, it puts great stress on your wrist (or elbow) and onto your shoulder. Injury to your wrist, elbow and shoulder could easily result. (no photo) The safe manner of falling is to avoid jarring or heavy contact onto the vulnerable wrist, elbow, or shoulder.

Instead of extending your arm, as though to catch yourself, put your arms out as you bend your knees . . .

129. . . . preparing to lower yourself onto your buttocks and roll . . .

130. . . . back onto your side, slapping the floor with your outstretched arm and hand as your upper body touches.

Study the photo carefully. Note that your head does not touch the floor, your weight is borne along the full length of your body from shoulder to buttocks so that there is no jolting impact at any vulnerable area. The essential action is gentle, rolling; avoid a thrusting, jarring action.

Practice this fall onto your right side and onto your left side.

127

Avoid this. 128

129

130

**Step-and-Turn Fall**

131. If you wish to allow your partner to put you onto the floor in practice of the wheeling-around takedowns, learn the step-turn fall. You can do this in solo practice by taking a step forward with your right foot as you extend your right arm (as though it were being pulled forward) . . . beginning a counterclockwise pivot.

132. As you continue the pivot, bend your knees so that you are lowering yourself to the floor . . .

133. . . . and as you touch the floor with your buttocks . . .

134. . . . continue the counterclockwise body turn so that you end the fall onto your left side with your head raised and your legs off the ground.

You should practice these falls slowly and carefully. An individual who is highly skilled in safety falling can be thrown down with considerable force onto a hard surface, but beginning students should not attempt fast falls.

131

132

133

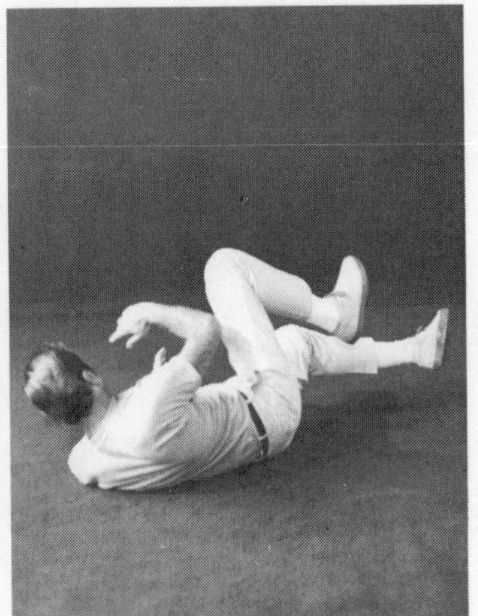

134

## SPIN-AROUNDS

If you can get around behind your assailant, you are less vulnerable to his intended assault; you can push him away, apply a simple takedown, or escape more easily.

Practice the spin-arounds in conjunction with a blocking or parrying action.

### Arm Spin-Around

135. Slash or block the reaching or hitting arm . . .

136. . . . and grip it with the same hand you use for blocking; using his forward movement to help your action, pull him forward, and then . . .

137. . . . sharply around so that you are behind him . . .

138. . . . and can complete your defense with appropriate hand and foot blows, or takedown.

You can use the arm spin-around without coming within hitting range of your assailant.

135

136

137

138

**Body Spin-Around**

**139**. Block or slash at your partner's reaching arms, and without hesitation . . .

139

140

141

**140.** . . . begin the spin-around by thrusting at his left shoulder with your right hand as you push at the back of his right shoulder with your left hand, using a snappy action . . .

**141.** . . . to turn him counterclockwise, in position for a takedown, or other suitable ending.

Practice the spin-around counterclockwise and clockwise to determine which seems most comfortable for you. The most efficient spin-around is executed with the help of momentum of the adversary's body movement. The spin-around will be less efficient if applied against the strong line.

## TAKEDOWNS

It is thrilling to watch spectacular throwing in movie fight scenes; it is exciting to watch sport judo matches in which the throwing techniques are executed in an amazing display of seemingly effortless style. For practical defense, the throwing techniques are not feasible. The high degree of technical skill needed to achieve throwing ability and the constant, ongoing practice needed to maintain this skill are factors which eliminate judo throws for basic self-defense.

There are so many modern assault situations in which a judo throw would not be possible and many situations in which a judo throw would be inappropriately violent. Can you imagine responding to unpleasant horseplay by flinging the annoying person down onto the ground?

Sometimes, putting an assailant onto the ground gives you time advantage—extra seconds in which to make your escape. Sometimes, it is necessary, for psychological reasons, to put an assailant onto the ground to signal that the assault has ended.

The takedowns which follow are simple, practical methods of putting an assailant onto the ground. These are not contest-style throws; they would not be permitted in judo matches; they are not exciting enough to be used in movie fight scenes—but they do the job!

Applying the principle of going-with, or working against the weak line, you would use a back trip or back takedown against an adversary who is vulnerable in that direction—not against an adversary moving forward; you would use a front trip against an adversary moving forward. Or, you can move the assailant to put him in poor balance, and then apply the trip in the direction of his weak line.

**Back Takedown**

142. You have weakened him with hand and foot blows and then wheeled him around. Grip his shoulder, or hair, with one hand and place your foot into the back of his knee. For safety practice, place your other hand at his far shoulder.

143. As you pull back with your arms, push with your foot. If your partner stands in a normal stance, you will see how little effort is needed to pull him back off balance. You can see how easy it would be to put him on the ground if you had used a vigorous kick into the back of his knee as you pulled back sharply with your hand.

144. It is not necessary to complete the action down to the ground, but if your partner loses his balance ease him down by maintaining your hand grip.

Avoid positioning yourself directly behind your partner. You should not be in the line of his fall. You want to avoid being pulled down as he goes onto the ground.

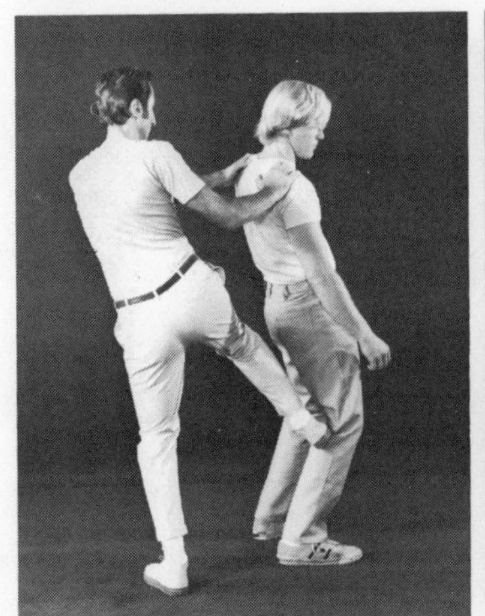

142

143

144

145

146

**Back Leg-Trip**

**145.** In practice, with your partner, place your right hand at his chest and grip his upper right arm with your left hand; extend your right leg and place your right foot so that it crosses both his legs, as shown. Push back gently: You are working against his weakest line of balance and it will take very little effort to put him off balance. In defense use, a vigorous push at his chest as you place your leg behind his legs to put him onto the ground with relatively little effort.

**146.** The same back trip could be effected using a heel-of-palm thrust up under his chin to trip him back over your leg.

For practice with your partner, it is not necessary to take him onto the ground. For safety, maintain a firm grip on his arm to help ease him down if he loses his balance completely.

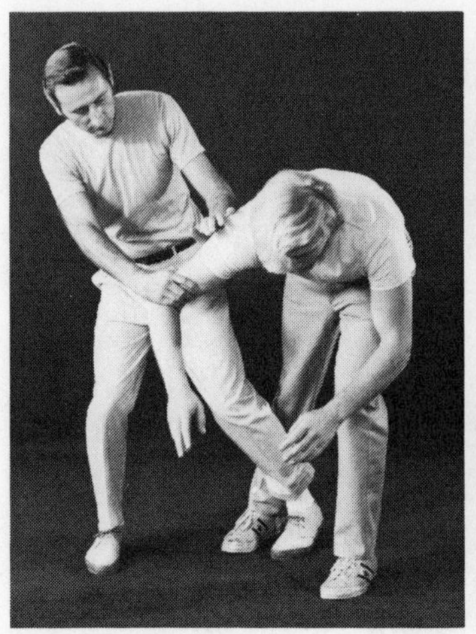

147

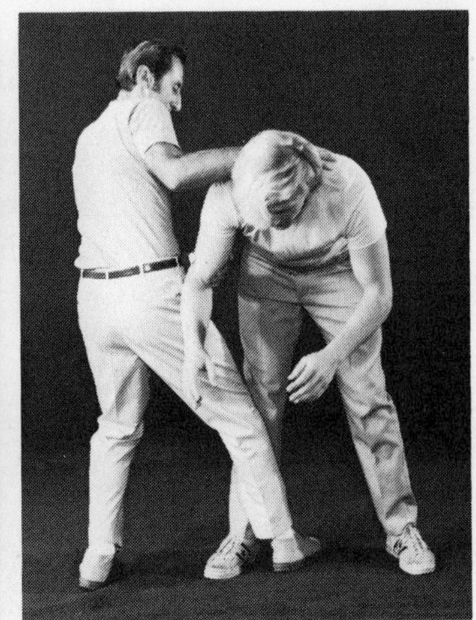

148

**Leg Blocks**

A front trip can be applied if you are at the side of an assailant or facing him.

**147.** Place your leg in front of his leg, as shown, as you push him forward to trip across your leg. Grip your practice partner's arm firmly to avoid thrusting him on the ground.

**148.** Facing your partner, place your leg in front of his leg and push him so that he trips over your extended leg.

Right arm action is important; in both instances, your right arm pulls or pushes him forward sharply.

**Over-The-Hip Wheeling Throw**

This technique is adapted from a judo throw, but does not require the same degree of technical precision that would be needed to apply a throw in contest. In a judo match, the opponent is not assaulting, he is trying to earn a point by executing a throw; he knows that the opponent player is also trying to execute a throw and he is therefore ready to cope with throwing attempts. In self-defense, your assailant should not know what you intend to do and will be less ready to cope—more vulnerable to the throw. This is not a stylish throw, but it can be used to put an assailant on the ground.

149. For practice, work very carefully with your partner; he neither assists nor resists your actions. Go through the motions of this technique in fairly slow motion.

Face your partner; grip his right arm with your left hand and as you begin to turn counterclockwise, slide your right arm around his waist.

150. When you have turned so that your right hip is in front of his right side, begin to wheel his body around, so that he . . .

151. . . . falls over your hip . . .

152. . . . and down and around in front of you. Your arms and upper body make a continuous counterclockwise wheeling movement to effect the throw. Do *not* fling your partner down onto the ground; by maintaining your grip around his waist and on his arm, you can ease him down.

149

150

151

152

**Trip-And-Wheel Takedown**

The trip-and-wheel takedown is an advanced technique, more difficult than the foregoing trips.

153. Standing in front of your partner, with your back to him, place your right arm around his waist and grip his right arm with your left hand. Extend your right leg and place your right foot close to his right foot, as shown, so that your leg crosses his, your left leg is somewhat bent.

154. Keeping your right foot in place, wheel him around in front of you, pulling with your left arm and wheeling your upper body counterclockwise . . .

155. . . . and follow through so that he falls around your leg and body.

156. Maintain your grip on his arm and waist so that you can ease him down onto the ground.

Work carefully with your practice partner; do not fling him down. He does not offer resistance; it is as though you had taken him by surprise, which would be the case in self-defense, and allows his body to move through the actions neither helping nor resisting your movements.

153

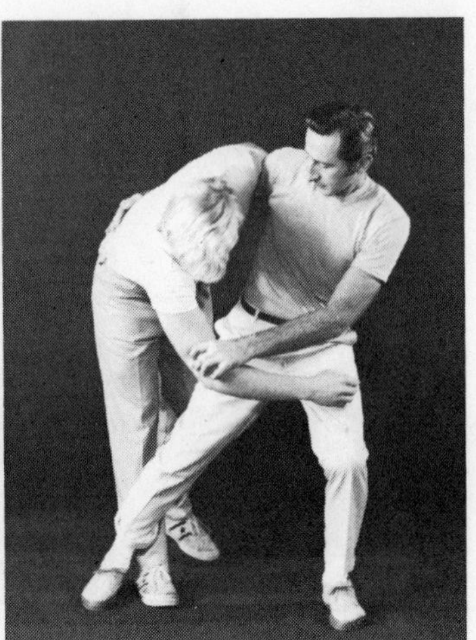

154

155

156

157

158

159

160

**Kick-Back Trip**

**157.** Facing your partner, take a deep step with your left foot, placing it six or eight inches away from his right foot, as shown; grip his left shoulder with your right hand and his right upper arm with your left hand.

158. As you pull forward with your left hand and back and around with your right hand, swing your fully-extended right leg up and back to hit his leg at the calf. When your leg makes contact with his, it should be calf-to-calf.

159. Follow through with your swinging-leg action and continue the pulling-pushing arm action . . .

160. . . . and maintain your grips on your partner to avoid flinging him down onto the ground.

**Forward Takedown**

161. An efficient action is one which takes the greatest advantage of your assailant's movements. This forward takedown would be the proper response to your attempt to use a takedown, as shown, and your action causes the assailant to fall forward.

162. Use his forward momentum to aid your action. Continue pushing into his knee with your foot, but push him forward to put him on the ground.

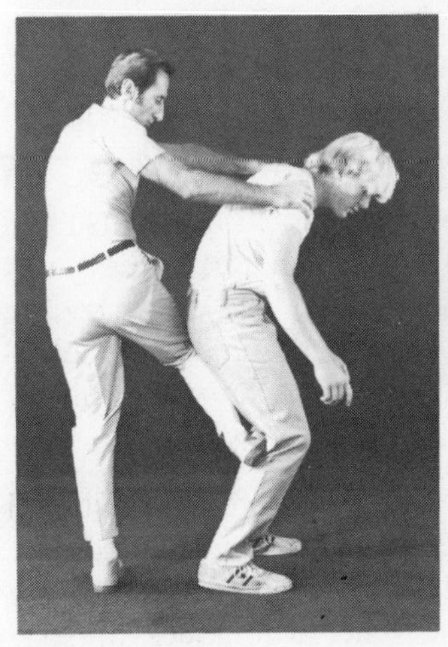

161

162

# PART THREE

## RESTRAINTS: HOLDS & LOCKS

The need for the average person to apply restraints is limited. Ordinarily, the prudent individual does not attempt to capture an assailant. The duty of the lay citizen is not the same as the duty of the professional who must take an offender into custody or keep an individual in custody.

There are, however, situations which confront individuals who are not policemen or institutional guards, but who might nevertheless, find it necessary to restrain a hostile, aggressive person.

As only a few examples of what I am talking about, if you are a teacher or bartender who has the responsibility of stopping fights or if you have a potentially violent (possibly self-destructive) person in your household, it would be prudent to know some restraining methods.

The most complicated of the holds and locks of jiu jitsu and aikido are out of the question for functional use; it takes years of training and practice to master them. They are dazzling when demonstrated by a highly-skilled person, but the seemingly effortless movements of the expert are the result of endless hours of effort.

The holds and locks which I have adapted from the traditional aikido and jiu jitsu repertoire of restraint techniques are those which many of my students have learned with relative ease. But, unlike some of the other techniques of self-defense, holds and locks do require some regular, continuing practice if you wish to maintain functional skill. If you are in a situation where the necessity of restraint is a possibility, then you would do well to learn a few holds and practice them from time to time.

For safety in practice with your partner, he acts as a passive model. If he offers resistance, there is a possibility of injury. Remind him to use the safety tapping signal if he feels excessive pain. Remember that you are not trying to *prove* techniques, you are simply learning them!

**Natural & Un-Natural Grips**

163. The natural grip is made by reaching forward as though to shake hands. Your thumb is at the top of the grip.

164. An un-natural grip is made by reaching forward with your hand turned so that your thumb is at the bottom of the grip.

163

164

**Basic Arm Bar**

165. Your partner, man shown right, extends his right arm; you grip his wrist with your right hand, using a natural grip.

166. Pulling his captured arm forward, and twisting it clockwise, you step around to place yourself at his side . . .

167. . . . and press down onto the back of his elbow with your left forearm.

This technique can be applied as a walk-along, with moderate force. You can step along briskly as you maintain the wrist twist and the pressure onto his elbow. Or, if appropriate, it can be applied forcefully to put an assailant onto the ground; instead of pressing down with your forearm, you would apply a smashing blow.

165

166

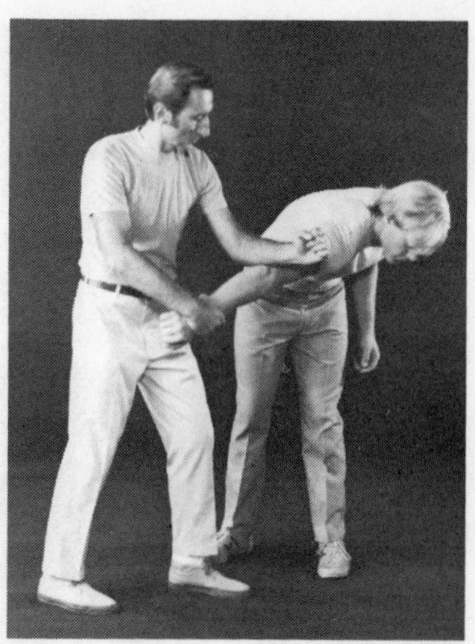

167

**Wrist-Twist Lock**

168. Grip his outstretched hand with both your hands; your thumbs are at the back of his hand and your fingers are into his palm.

168

169

170

**169.** Turn counterclockwise to put body weight into your action as you twist his captured hand up and back.

**170.** Follow through so that you are at his side, as shown, applying pressure against his captured wrist. You can place your leg behind his leg and lever him down to the ground, or you can walk him backward as you maintain pressure.

### Front Bent-Arm Lock

**171.** As your partner reaches toward you with his right hand, simulate a slash into the bend of his elbow with your left hand as you grip his wrist with your right hand.

**172.** Turning counterclockwise, raise his captured wrist, allowing it to turn within your grasp; your left hand slides under his captured arm and grips your own right wrist.

**173.** Levering your upper body around counterclockwise, apply pressure against his captured arm and wrist; walk him backward.

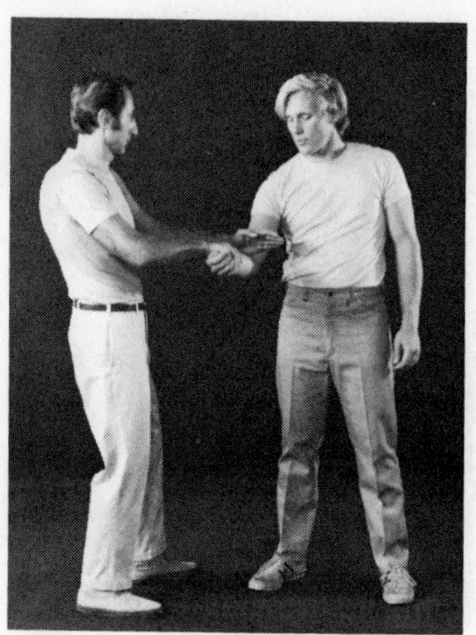

171

172

173

174

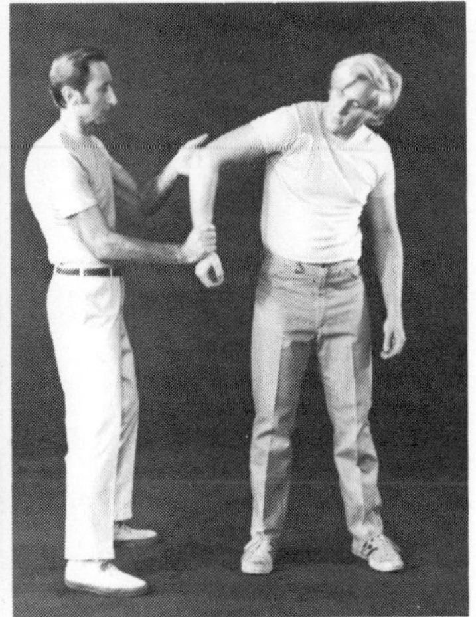

175

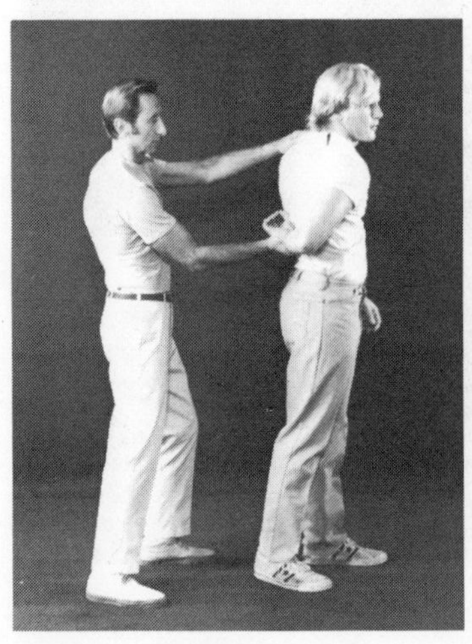

176

177

### Rear Bent-Arm Lock

174. Grip your partner's right wrist with your right hand, using a natural grip.

175. Hit at the outside of his elbow with your left hand, to bend his arm, as shown . . .

176. . . . and step around behind him as you twist his captured arm back and up. From this position you can place your left hand at his shoulder and push him forward as you continue the upward pressure on his wrist . . .

177. . . . or you can grip hair and continue pressure on his captured wrist as you walk him briskly forward.

### Wrist & Elbow Lock & Variations

178. Place your right hand against the back of your partner's right hand, as shown.

179. Grip his arm just above the elbow with your left hand as you begin to bend his captured hand.

178

179

180

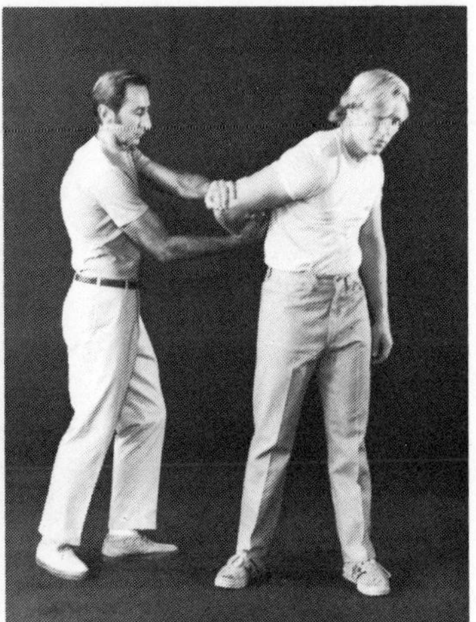

181

180. Maintain upward pressure against his wrist as you step around in back of him and push his elbow toward his wrist with your left hand. Maintaining pressure, you can walk him forward.

181. Or, you can thrust his captured hand up his back and walk him forward briskly from this position, maintaining pressure as you walk.

**Variation #1.**

182. From this position, your partner will draw his captured arm in and up.

183. Using the going-with principle, follow the action by pushing his elbow away from you and twisting his captured wrist in toward him and then up and back, as shown . . .

184. . . . and maintaining your pressure, walk him backward.

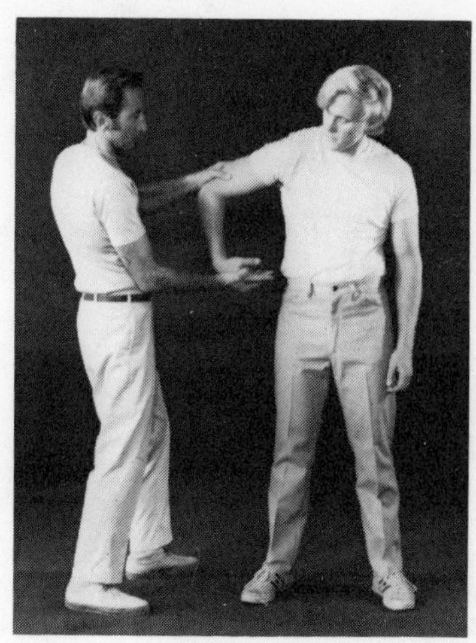

182

183

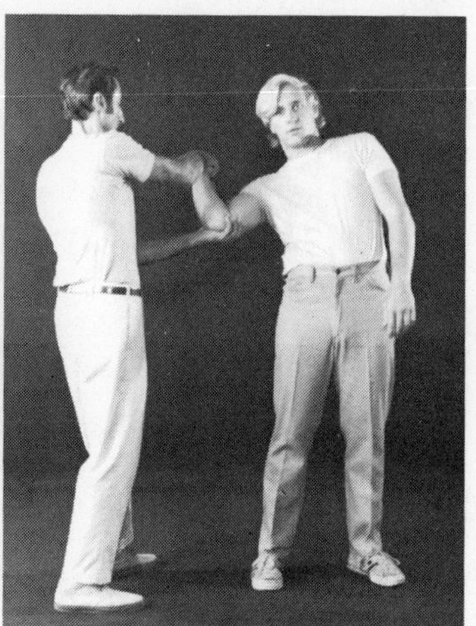

184

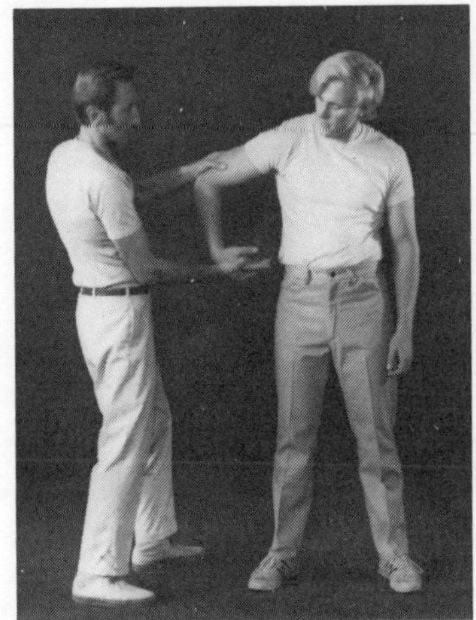

185

186

**Variation #2.**

**185.** From this position, your partner draws his captured arm in toward his body . . .

**186.** . . . you follow his action by pivoting clockwise, sliding your left hand under his arm and placing it at the back of his captured hand. Pulling back with both your hands, walk him forward, briskly.

# PART FOUR

## COMPLETE DEFENSES: On-Going Actions, Flexible Combinations

The two concepts which are fundamental to this method of self-defense are: flexible combinations of basic actions and on-going defense.

Both of these concepts contradict the old-style karate, jiu jitsu and aikido methods, which rely heavily on rigid series of "moves" in which the specific defense is a reaction to a specific attack.

### On-Going Defense

Whether or not you have reached a high level of skill and sophistication in using techniques of self-defense, you can apply the concept of on-going by simply repeating the defense action as long as required. If only one technique comes to mind, use that action over and over. The number of actions required to complete a defense will vary with the situation. Most defenses are completed with very few actions—just enough to demonstrate a refusal to play the part of helpless victim.

When you realize that you can make your defense on-going from the very first day of practice, you can eliminate the question "What do I do next?" If you know one or two defense techniques, you use them as on-going defense for as long as is necessary.

### Combining the Actions

Repeating one or two defense techniques as required makes an on-going defense. Combining three or four techniques in a flexible manner and repeating them as necessary, makes a more sophisticated, effective defense. The ability to use the basic material in a flexible way, eliminates the need to recall a specific series of "moves" and frees you from the rigid pattern of action-reaction. The concepts of on-going and flexible are more realistic than the set-pattern defenses. You cannot depend on an assailant to perform a set pattern of assault moves to which you respond in a set pattern of defense moves.

Remember that you are practicing concepts; you can begin practice of both concepts in slow motion. Practice partners take turns, and the partner playing the role of assailant acts as a reference target only; as you gain assurance and experience in practicing the on-going combinations, you can speed up the actions and the partner playing the role of assailant can provide reaction moves to which you respond in an appropriate manner.

Try to avoid getting into the habit of repeating the same series of actions. You might develop a favored sequence, which is fine, but do not rely on set, rigid patterns.

Observe the safety rules, carefully. In this, as in any of the other practice procedures, you need not hurt each other to gain the objective of the practice.

The combinations which are illustrated are merely examples. The illustrated examples are intended to get you started. After you practice the example combinations, you make up your own combinations. If you know ten actions and use only four of those ten in any possible combination, you can make more than five thousand different combinations of on-going defenses!

187

188

**SIMPLE COMBINATIONS**

**187.** Begin by combining hand blows in a one-two rhythm. As, for instance, a heel-of-palm blow up under the nose . . .

**188.** . . . followed by an edge-of-hand slash into the side of the neck.

Repeat the same combination, but reverse the order of the blows. Repeat the combination using your right hand for the slashing blow and your left hand for the palm blow.

With this simple combination, you can begin to see the advantage of flexible applications for a small group of basic techniques.

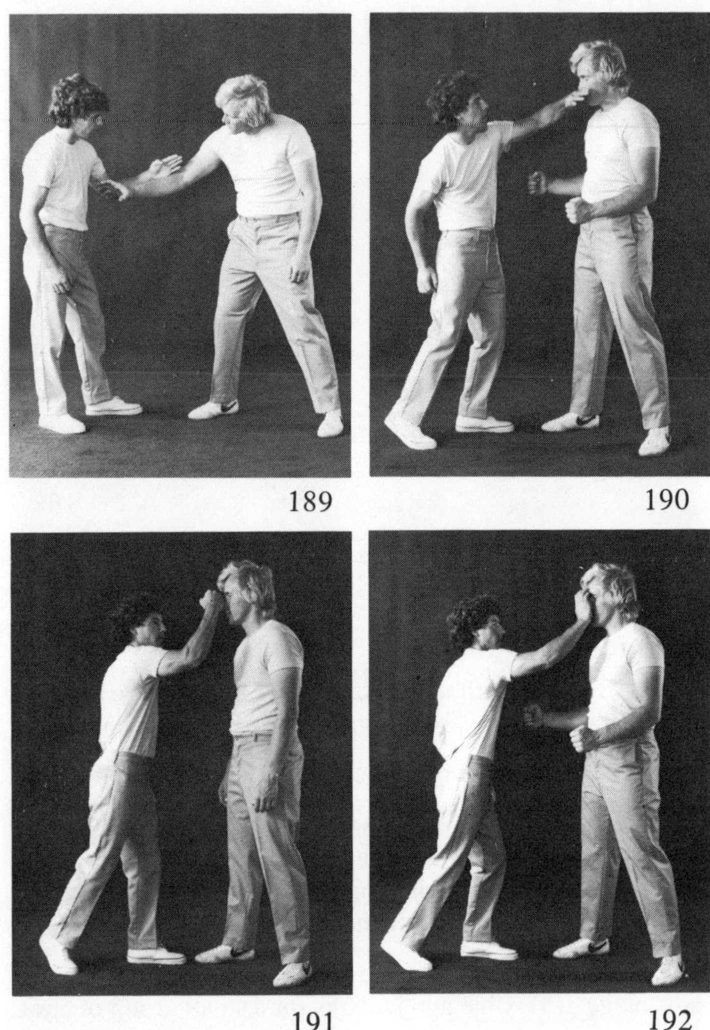

189 190

191 192

**189.** Next, try combinations of two hand blows, using the same hand for the two blows. As, for instance, a slashing blow onto the forearm . . .

**190.** . . . followed by a slashing upward blow under the nose, using your left hand for both blows.

Practice this one-two combination with your right hand.

**191.** Practice a one-two combination beginning with a right-handed hammer blow onto the nose . . .

**192.** . . . and follow with an open-handed thrust into the face with the same hand.

Practice this combination with your left hand.

## BLOCK/PARRY COMBINATIONS

Practice the parries as one-two combinations.

**193.** Right man is prepared to block two blows, using the various techniques. This procedure may be practiced with moderate contact, but there is no need for rough work.

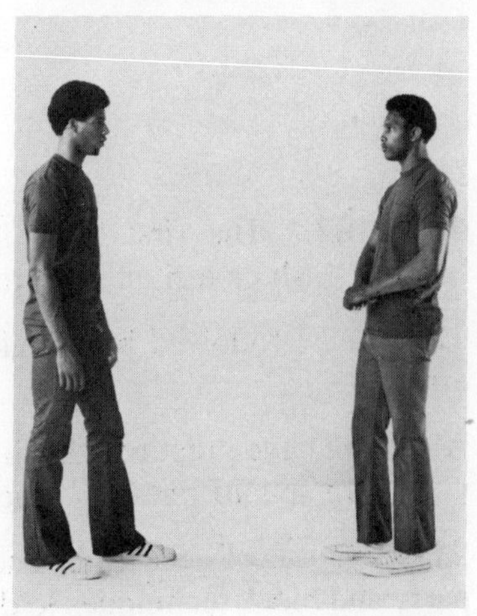

193

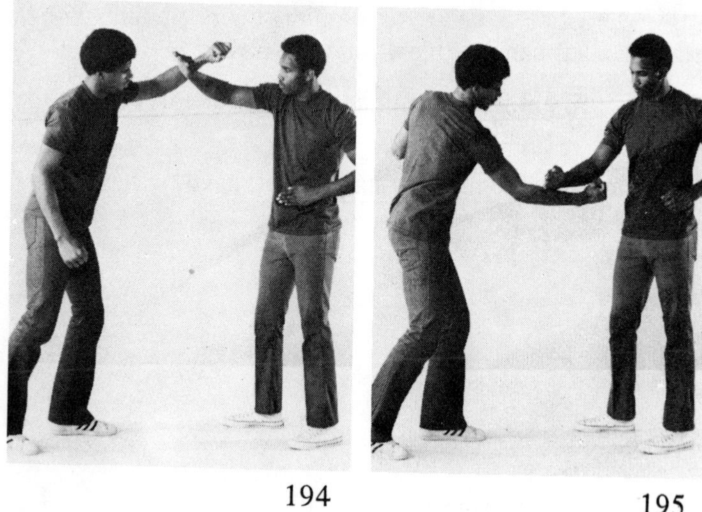

194 195

**194.** The first block is a slashing, upward action . . .

**195.** . . . followed by a downward slash, using the same hand.

**196, 197.** The first blow is a cross-body, high right-handed slash or a right forearm block/parry . . .

**198.** . . . followed by a high forearm block with the left arm.

After you have practiced the illustrated combinations, make your own sets of one-two blocks and parries.

Alternate use of your right and left hands; practice all the parry and block techniques to discover the few you are most comfortable with and then emphasize those to develop the ability to respond spontaneously, using your favorite parries.

When you feel fairly comfortable with one-two combinations, expand them into four-count combinations, first by repeating the one-two blows, and, as you develop more skill, combine four different hand blows, including parries.

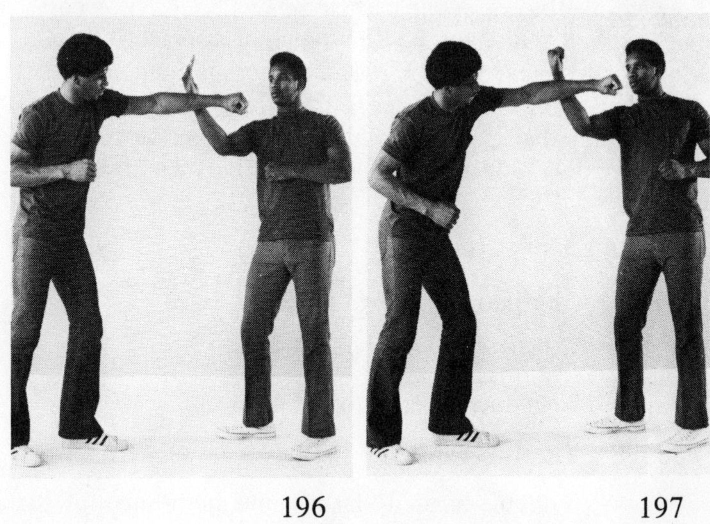

196 197

198

### Six-count Practice Procedure

First, practice the six-count series as illustrated, then make your own combinations.

Practice for smooth, flowing gestures, without hesitations between the blows. Your partner acts as a reference point, only. Simulate the blows without making contact, but make vigorous gestures. Smooth, on-going work is more important than speed. If you work too fast, at first, your movements will be irregular. You can count in time as you do this series and work only as fast as you can deliver blows in rhythmical sequence.

**199.** Slash/block low . . .

**200.** . . . hit into the side of the neck . . .

**201.** . . . slash down onto the nose . . .

**202.** . . . hammer blow onto the nose . . .

**203.** . . . heel-of-palm into the face . . .

**204.** . . . double-handed slashes into both sides of the neck.

199

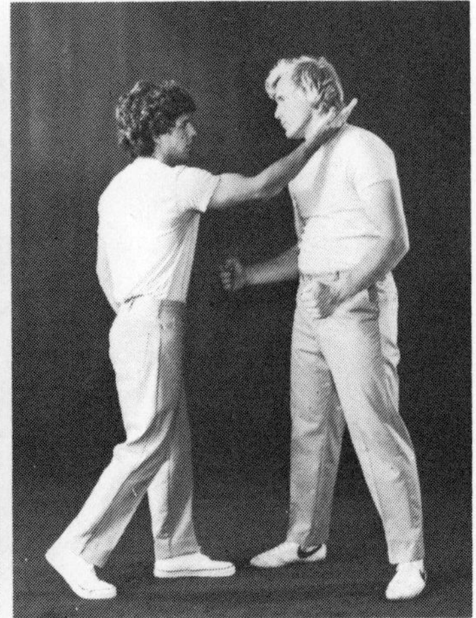

200

201

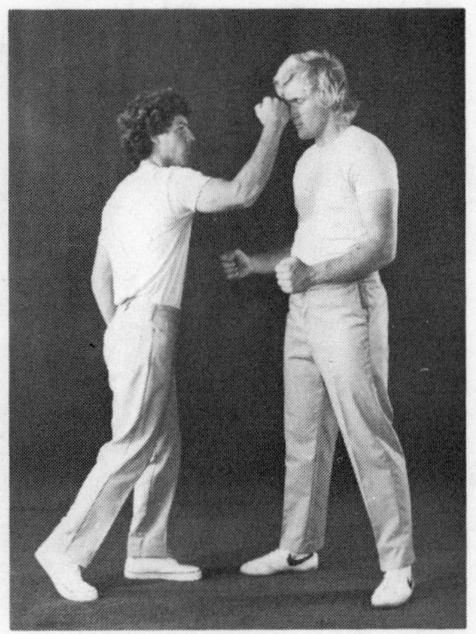

202

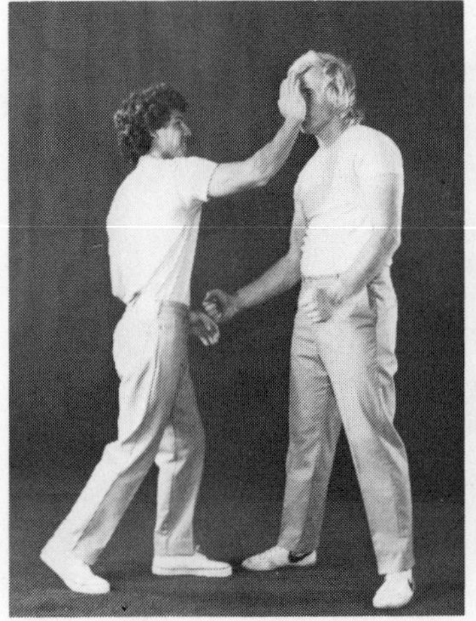

203

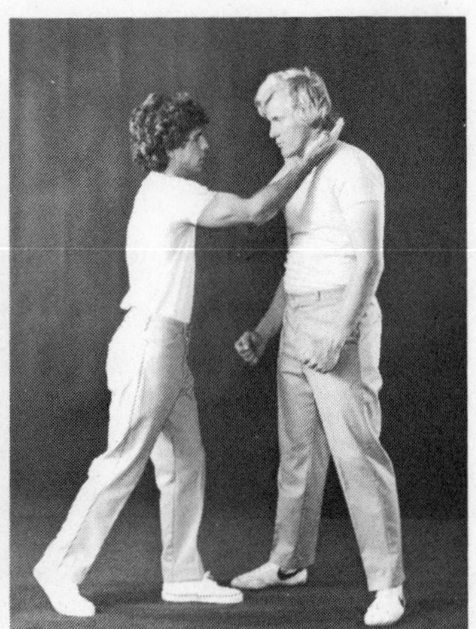

204

Now proceed to improvise your own series, working for smooth-flowing, rhythmical alternation of left and right, high and low, hand blows and parries.

205

206

## KICKING COMBINATIONS

**205.** Begin to practice for on-going kicks with one-two combinations . . .

**206.** . . . alternating left and right kicks.

Practice on-going kicking techniques by delivering a series of kicks with the same foot. Practice the snap kick and the stamp kick; practice left and right kicks; extend the series until you can comfortably deliver a six-count series without loss of balance.

207

208

**KICK & HIT COMBINATIONS**

The next step is to make combinations of hand and foot blows. Think in tactical terms of alternating high and low target areas for most effective defense.

207. Start with one-two actions, blocking high . . .

208. . . . and kicking without hesitation.

Make your own combinations of one-two hit-and-kick combinations, using all the techniques you can, in as many combinations as you can think of.

**Block-Kick-Hit Combination**

First, practice the illustrated three-count series of different actions.

209. Slash/block the arm . . .

209

210. . . . and kick, without hesitation . . .

211. . . . and deliver a heel-of-palm blow into the face.

Improvise other combinations of parry-kick-hit, and emphasize the use of both hands and both feet. Avoid total reliance on your strong side.

210

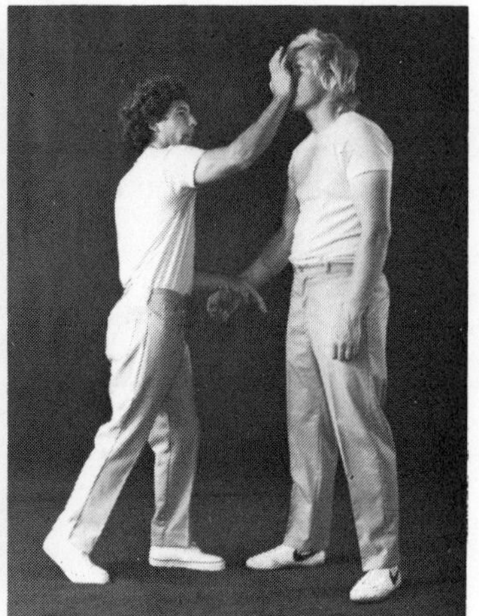

211

212

### Kick-Hit-Trip Combination

212. Then, proceed to practice combinations which include a kick . . .

213. . . . and hand blow . . .

214. . . . and an ending takedown or trip.

213

214

Observe all the safety rules carefully. Work for smooth, rhythmical actions, without hesitations between the techniques.

Make up your own combinations, using as many techniques as you know in various, different ways.

215

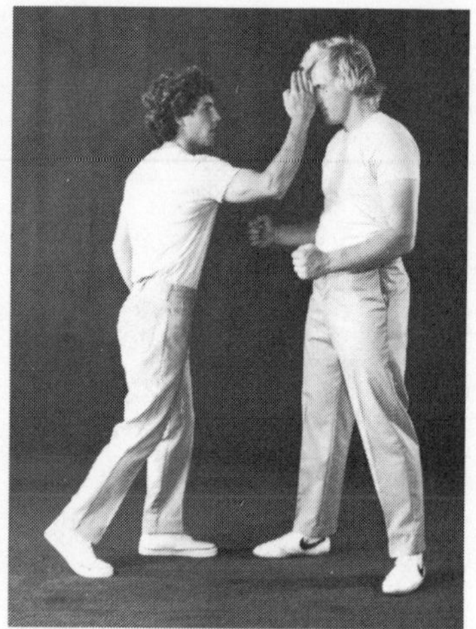

216

**DOUBLE-TRIPLE COMBINATIONS**

The double and triple combinations are practice procedures. If you can develop the ability to use more than one blow at a time, your defense is considerably more sophisticated than if you use blows one at a time. For functional self-defense, you do not need to be able to use doubles and triples, but if you practice them, they will increase your single-blow efficiency.

Begin by practicing a double blow, followed by a single blow.

215. Simultaneous slap/parry and kick . . .

216. . . . followed by a hand blow, for instance.

Make up your own combinations of double actions followed by a single hit or kick.

Then, practice consecutive double actions.

217. A slash and kick, using left hand and foot . . .

218. . . . followed by a hand and foot blow using your right hand and foot.

Then proceed to practice triples, using double-handed blows with each kick.

219. Practice a triple action using the edge-of-shoe snap kick with two hand blows . . .

220. . . . and follow with a second set of simultaneous triple actions, reversing the position of your hands and kicking with your other foot. Invent your own series of triples.

217

218

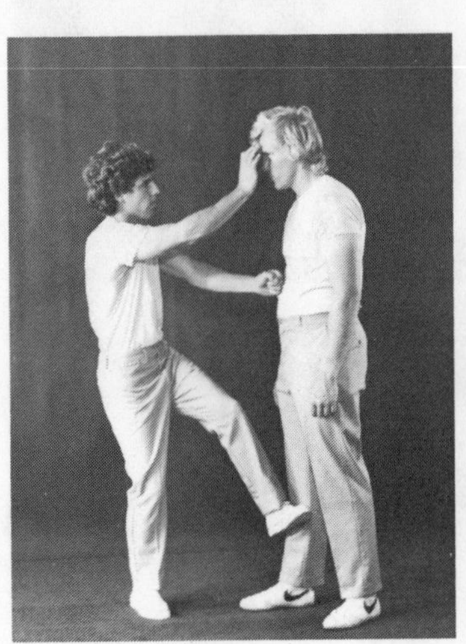

219

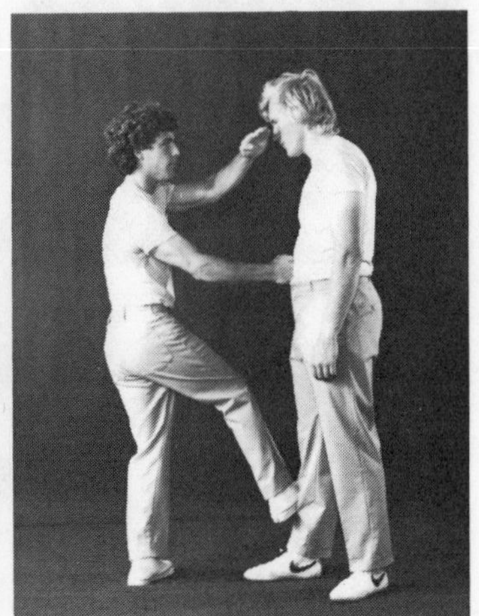

220

**COMPLETE COMBINATIONS**

First, practice the combinations illustrated. Work for smooth, rhythmical, on-going actions.

221. Block high . . .

222. . . . block low . . .

223. . . . kick . . .

224. . . . hit . . .

225. . . . spin-around . . .

226. . . . ready for a takedown.

221

222

223

224

225

226

### Block-Grip-Kick-Spin Combination

This combination includes the tactical device of stiffening your arms to immobilize him, briefly. Against someone stronger than you, the immobilization would be very brief, but it is useful.

227. Slash-block one arm . . .

228. . . . and then the other . . .

229. . . . grip his arms and stiffen your arms to immobilize him briefly . . .

230. . . . so that you can kick . . .

231. . . . twice . . .

232. . . . and spin him around, in position for a takedown.

227

228

229

230

231

232

Finally, the objective of combination practice is to gain the ability to make *any* appropriate combination of hand and foot blows appropriate to the situation and complete the defense, if necessary, by using an appropriate takedown or restraining hold, if that is the prudent thing to do.

Your first attempts at making your own combinations will take some time and thinking. Do your thinking before you practice. Thinking about what you might do is your mental rehearsal. At first, you will have to plan your combinations. Partners help each other by pointing out ways of improving the combinations. Make your suggestions in a positive manner. For instance, if your partner consistently fails to use both his hands for hand blows, tell him to use his left hand (or right hand) more. In general, if you tell him what to do, rather than what he has done wrong, you encourage and help, rather than criticize and discourage.

It takes some practice to arrive at a level of competence at which you are able to improvise defense combinations without first thinking of a model series so that you can respond spontaneously with varied, on-going defense actions which are appropriate to the situation. That is the ultimate objective of practical self-defense.

# PART FIVE

## SELF-DEFENSE FOR WOMEN & CHILDREN

You cannot have come this far in the book without realizing that my view of self-defense departs from the traditional in a number of ways; among them is the concept that self-defense is for those who are *least* able to acquire expert standing as fighters.

Women and children are uncritically relegated to the category of helpless individuals. Women are defined as unable to progress from helplessness to self-sufficiency simply because they are women. Different goals are set for little boys and for little girls. Regardless of temperament, physical capacity, or size, little boys are expected to be natural fighters, whereas little girls are expected to be naturally and unchangeably helpless.

At least that is how it was last year. This year, we might be forced to give up some cherished myths and look at reality.

The false alternatives which are popularly accepted as choices, are a particular impediment to women who want to learn self-defense. The myth of female helplessness is joined to the myth of male aggression. This is how the argument goes: Since women are naturally passive and since one has to be a fierce, aggressive fighter to be able to defend oneself, it follows, of course, that women cannot learn the manly art of self-defense, only men can.

The myth of male "natural" aggression is the other side of this fake coin. If all women were "naturally" unable to learn self-defense because of their passivity and all men were "naturally" aggressive and competent to fight, there would be no need for self-defense instruction for men and all such classes for women would be unsuccessful. The reality is quite different. Men are the major consumers of books and lessons in the field. As individuals, hundreds of them have admitted to me, personally, that they felt inadequate and helpless. After some instruction in self-defense, they felt more confident and assured. Women have *exactly* the same experience as men, with respect to self-defense lessons. They feel helpless and inadequate before taking instruction and they feel more assured and self-reliant after taking instruction.

Neither the men nor the women I teach become aggressive, fierce fighters; they become more assertive and confident and less likely to become victims.

**She Can Do It!**

The man who insists that his wife, friend, daughter, girl-child cannot learn to defend herself, may not realize this, but he is clinging to the myth of "man as the natural fighter" because it makes him feel, by his membership in this group, that he is superior to all members of that other group —females. There are six times as many assaults against men as there are assaults against women. It is neither men nor women who are the most helpless, it is the unprepared, of either sex.

Since self-defense for girls and women is not preparation to engage in "fair" fights with men, but is preparation to minimize the possibility of assault and teach them how to avoid the role of passive victim, women can and do learn self-defense very well.

If a man is confident enough of his own worth as a person, he will be able to help a girl or woman learn self-defense by playing the role of assailant without having to "win." The man who cannot do this is not a good partner for a woman who wants to learn self-defense. It is my experience that the more confidence a man has in his real worth, the less he has to rely on group worth. Whenever I encounter a man who makes fun of women who want to defend themselves, I feel sorry for him; he has to feel superior to someone else because he is uncertain of himself.

#### What to Learn?

How many techniques a woman should learn for self-defense will depend, as it does with men, on the level of skill she wants to reach and on her individual concerns, preferences and style.

There is a suggested basic lesson plan for girls and women in the appendix section of this book. But that is simply a guide and not a rigid formula. There are women who are capable of and interested in learning all or practically all of the defense techniques which are in the text; others may wish to learn the fewest possible actions for basic instruction.

The environment in which a woman or girl learns self-defense is as important as the number of techniques she practices and the level of skill she achieves.

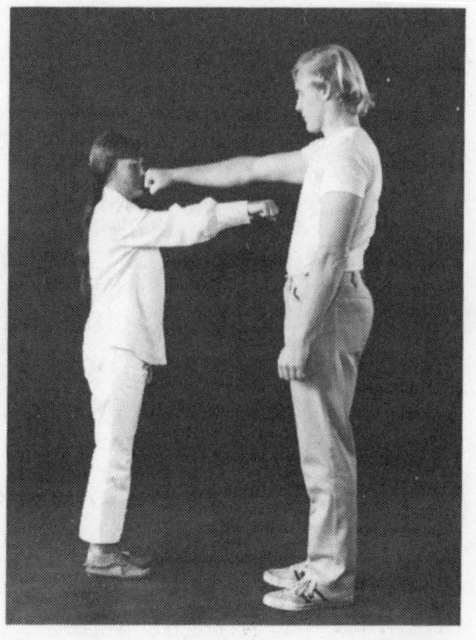

233

**233**. Traditional approaches and traditional techniques will not be effective. The traditional hand blows, whether they are karate or boxing, will not be appropriate. The concept of self-defense as a contest is not appropriate. The photo makes the point, clearly.

234

235

**234.** If she tries to use strength alone, it is ineffective; she cannot pull herself free. This photo and the following one illustrate the difference between effective and ineffective techniques. Using her fists to pound on his chest is ineffective.

**235.** With the same technique, using the same amount of force, she uses the edge of her fist and pounds onto his nose, convincing him that she is capable of orderly and practical defense.

### Partners Must Help

**236.** Be a good, helpful practice partner. Don't try to show off your superiority; you are stronger than the woman you will work with. A real assailant would be, too. Except that in actual self-defense, she would really kick and hit, instead of simulating the gestures of hitting and kicking. When she hits up with her elbow and scrapes along your shin, in simulation, react as though she had done the real defense. Use your imagination! Imagine what it would feel like to get whacked in the face with an elbow and kicked in the shin . . .

**237.** . . . and then have your instep stomped on.

**238.** Undoubtedly, your grip would relax enough to allow her to hit again with her elbow, and kick again, if necessary, to effect release.

236

237

238

Practicing with a man or woman partner is not practice to "prove" that the defenses are effective; if it were, you would have to allow full-contact hand and foot blows. The objective of practicing with a partner is to rehearse success. The assailant partner does his share by playing the role "as if." Encourage positive attitudes and remind your partner that other people no larger or stronger than she is have learned and been successful with these defense actions.

It is particularly important that you play the "as if" role when you're helping a girl or woman practice defenses against assaults which seem especially threatening. The series of actions for coping with the back choke, for instance, is not highly complicated, and the feeling of helplessness which most women bring to this situation is a serious impediment to learning the defense. You must reassure and help her. You can do this by offering very little resistance to her defense actions the first few times.

239. Your grip should be moderately strong . . .

240. . . . allowing her to turn her head, grip your arm and kick, without undue restraint . . .

241. . . . and permit her to escape . . .

242. . . . and complete the defense as shown.

After you have practiced several times, you can grip with more realism (but always avoid choking against the windpipe) and react to her defense actions when they are performed with vigor and spirit.

Work slowly. Make your criticisms positive rather than negative. Instead of saying, for instance, "You are not kicking hard enough," convert the same statement into a positive instruction to "Kick harder."

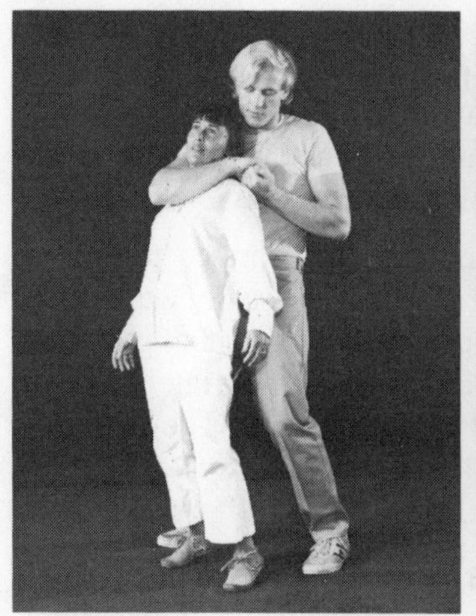
239

240

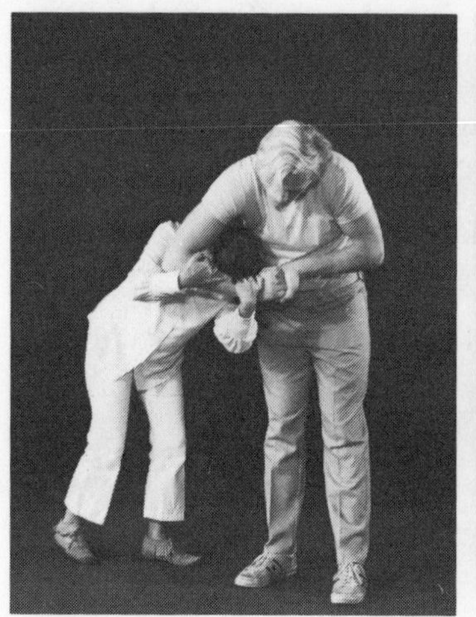
241

242

**THE ASSERTIVE "NO!"**

Improvise and rehearse the possible responses to non-assaultive, but unwelcome advances. The lack of preparation to cope with an unwelcome advance in a calm, assured manner results in passivity which is confusing.

An ineffective or negative response is interpreted to mean "This woman is just pretending to resist; she really wants me to use more persuasion." Because most women and girls do not know how to resist sexual advances appropriately, they behave in an embarrassed and confused way. The embarrassment further complicates the situation because they do not appear to be serious.

When you are working with a woman partner to help her achieve the feeling of competence she needs, encourage her to sound and look convincing as she does these simple defenses. She should be encouraged to express anger if she wants to, but the most important expression to convey is sincere determination to cope with the situation before it becomes more threatening and difficult to handle.

243. From a seated position, practice the finger-bending release against various types of grabbing.

244. A grinding or stamping down onto the instep is a convincing way of saying "Don't do that to me."

245. The edge-of-fist blow down onto the nose is as effective seated as standing.

246. The heel-of-palm thrust up under the nose or chin is useful close in.

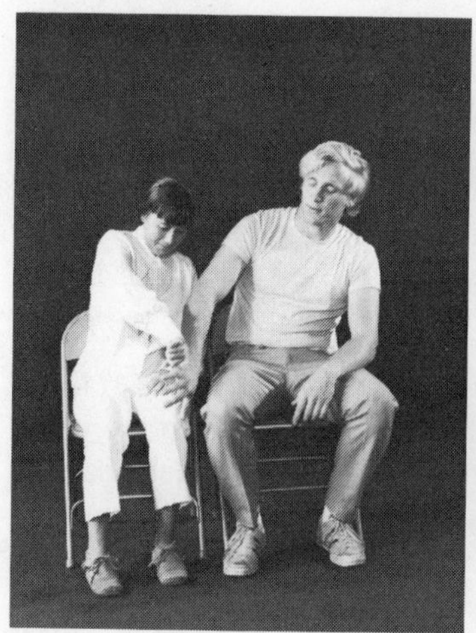
243

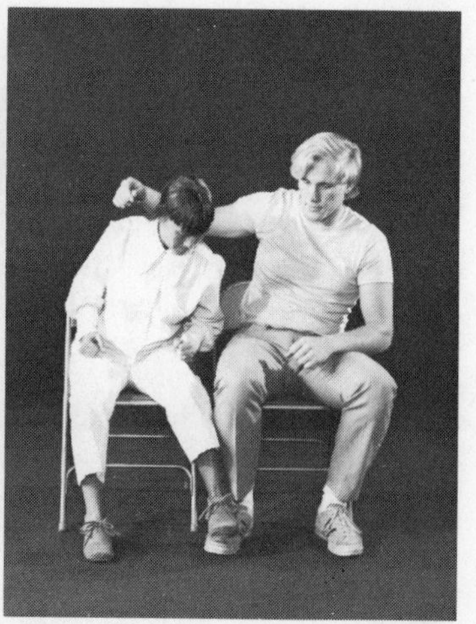
244

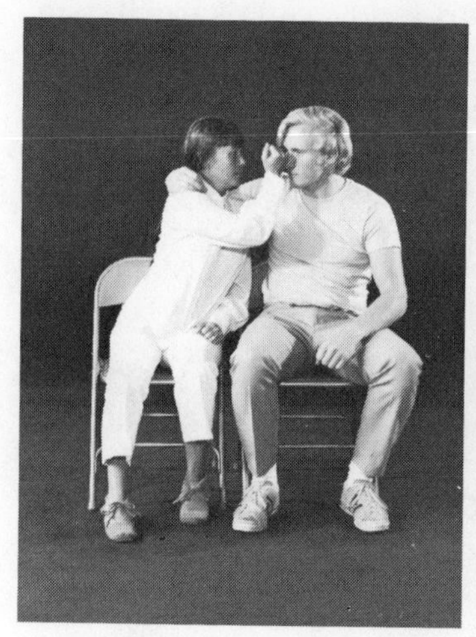
245

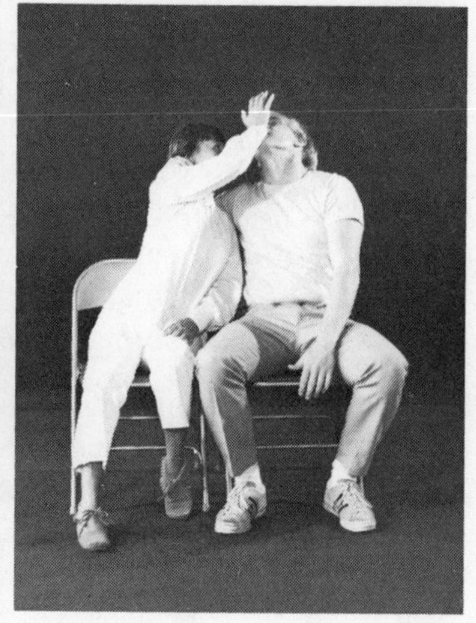
246

## DEFENSE FOR CHILDREN

During the eighteen years when I was teaching at my own school in Hollywood, children were a major group among my students. Most of the children who were brought in for lessons were boys, but I know that there were many girls who would have benefited from self-defense instruction if it had been made available to them, as it is beginning to be now.

Whether the child is large or small, male or female, is of little consequence in the teaching and learning of practical self-defense. For children, as for adults, the greatest accomplishment is not the acquisition of fighting skill, but the achievement of self-respect, self-reliance and self-confidence.

To teach, or help a child learn self-defense, you do not need advanced skill or a belt degree. You need patience, consideration and sensitivity.

Thousands of children were brought into my school for lessons. They were brought in by mothers and by fathers. Parents gave a variety of reasons for the child's inability to cope with bullies. One parent would say that the child was small for his age and couldn't deal with the bigger children. Another parent would say that the child was big for his age, and awkward, and this made him unable to cope. One parent would speculate that the boy was timid because he could not measure up to his father's superior physical skills; another would say that his child did not have physical skills because he did not have a strong father-image for a model.

Some parents would explain that the child would do nothing to defend himself because he feared that trying to defend himself would result in greater violence against him. Other parents would interpret passivity as fear of hurting an assailant.

Most of the reasons given by all these parents were in direct contradiction to the reasons given by other parents. The most frequent complaint among fathers was that their boys were babied by their mothers. The most frequent complaint made by the mothers was that their children had been intimidated by their fathers or deprived of a father through divorce.

With all the different circumstances of their lives, big or small, demanding father or protective mother, awkward or able, the overwhelming majority of children who were brought to my classes reported that they felt better after they had taken a short course of basic self-defense.

### The Real Problem

This certainly suggests that the real problem, the one which most of the parents had failed to consider, was lack of preparation to meet the emergency of assault. The common denominator was helplessness which resulted from not knowing what to do or how to do it.

Self-defense is neither automatic nor instinctive. Self-defense is learned. The aggressive child learns to fight easily, by imitation. The passive child must be taught carefully and consciously to avoid the role of victim. It is a mistake to think of self-defense as instinctive; if it were, everybody could do it.

There are many emergency situations for which we prepare children. We do not expect them to respond correctly, automatically, to the danger of fire; we give them fire drills. We do not expect children to respond correctly, automatically, to street signals; we teach them what to do. Though the procedures in each case are very easy, we know that they must be taught and practiced. Self-defense should be simple, but it is not automatic. Saying that your child cannot defend himself when he has never been taught how, is like complaining that your child cannot read before going to school.

If your passive child has never been permitted to rehearse successful, positive behavior in a simulated assault situation, it is unreasonable to expect positive behavior in the face of an actual threat of assault.

**Be Understanding**

Children who are afraid of bullies or timid about the possibility of physical aggression have two worries. They are afraid of the bully, but they also fear the contempt of their parents. To help a child learn self-defense, you must be sensitive to the child's feelings and not try to force your own feelings on the child.

The passive or timid child needs to be encouraged, not criticized. "I could do it, I don't know why you can't" is an abusive, hostile remark for a parent to make to a child. "I know that you can cope with this problem and I want to help you" is the kind of remark which is honestly supportive and positive.

Explain the rules of safety before you permit children to practice defense techniques. But make certain that the passive child is given ample opportunity to hit hard by using the training aids.

Emphasize practice of verbal and body-language assertion. Children enjoy play-acting and they are usually better at it than adults who have acquired inhibitions and lost a good measure of spontaneity.

If two children are practicing together, let them take turns defending and acting the bully partner.

Let them exaggerate and have fun.

247. The left child exaggerates the role of passive victim who cowers down in fear of the bully.

248. And she enjoys the assertive role. Very timid children need encouragement to play the assertive role properly. Make your suggestions positive and supporting. Avoid the negative sentences. If you are tempted to say "Your voice isn't loud and firm enough," transpose it to the positive, "Speak louder and look serious."

247

248

**What to Teach Children**

The number of techniques each child should learn will depend on individual need, temperament and interest.

There is a suggested lesson plan in the appendix section of this book, but it is intended as a guide, not as a rigid formula.

Go over the photos with the child or children you will be working with and let them have a choice in setting up the specific defenses to be practiced.

Emphasize, throughout, that prudent behavior is avoidance, rather than immediate use of physical defenses, whenever possible.

**Emphasize Safety**

It is depressingly discouraging for children who fear body contact to be hit or hurt in beginning sessions of self-defense. They ask, with compelling logic, why they should get hurt learning how not to get hurt?

Be very careful to explain that blows are "as if" blows and that they do not really hit each other, if two children are practicing together. If you are a parent practicing with a child, be cautious about how much contact you allow; I warn you that a nine-year-old child hitting with a fully-released blow can hurt you. Light contact might be permitted, but that is a matter for individual judgment and decision.

The simulated blows should be made in a spirited manner even though there is no actual contact. The photos show contact blows, so you should explain to the child that this is what it would look like if used for defense, and that it does not indicate practice procedures.

249. In the practice of the hair-pulling defense, include practice of a verbal command, such as "Let go of me," "Stop that," or other assertive phrases.

250. Then, if necessary, apply the physical defense action with spirit, starting with gripping the bully's wrist and pulling it toward her own head to reduce the pain . . .

251. . . . and kicking into the shin, first lightly, but if that does not effect release, again, with more force.

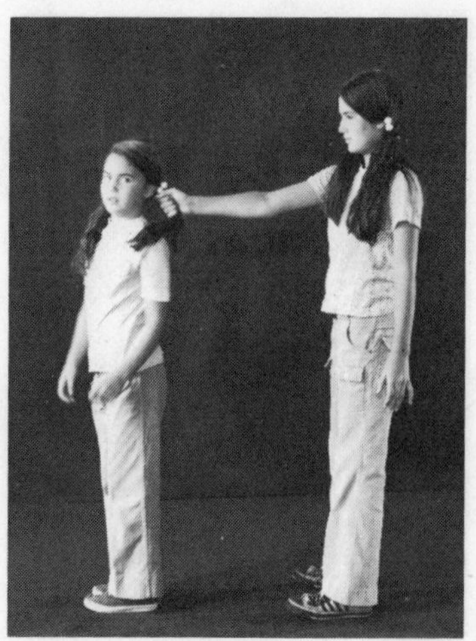

249

250

251

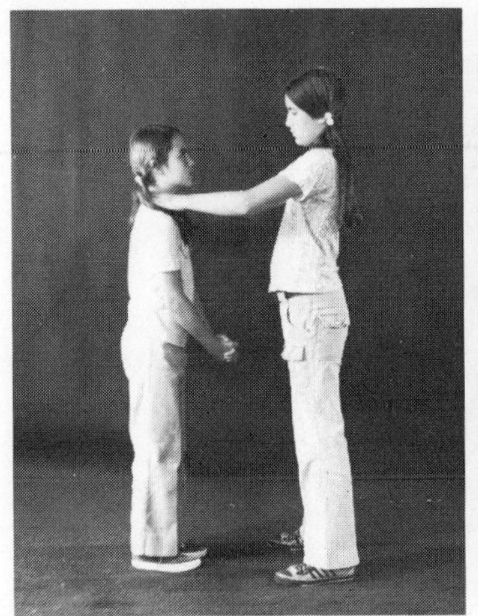

252

253

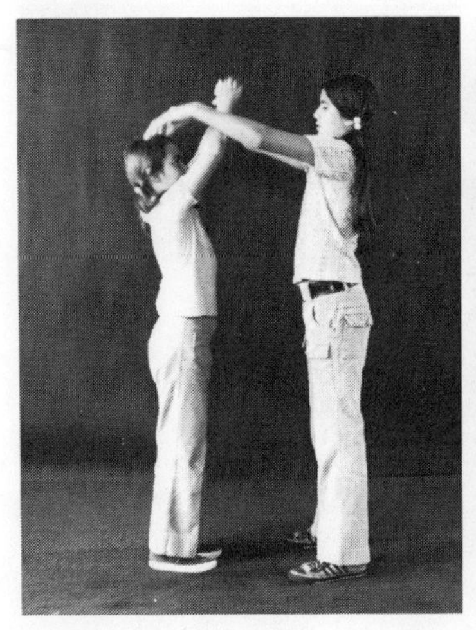

254

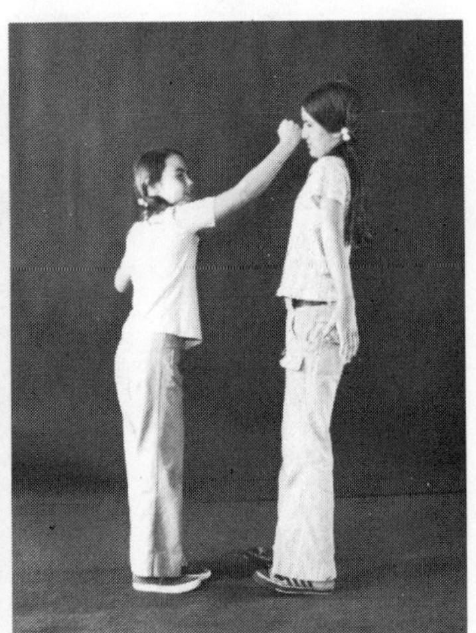

255

Against a shoulder grab or front choke, children might make light-contact slashing blows onto the assailant partner's forearms.

252. An alternate defense is made with clasped hands . . .

253. . . . thrust vigorously upward between the assailant's arms . . .

254. . . . with follow through to effect release.

255. And a fist-edge blow down onto the nose to complete the defense.

256. To demonstrate the various applications of a simple technique, such as the finger-bending release, the child might practice it against a one-handed arm grip.

257. And then proceed to practice it as part of the rear choke defense . . .

256

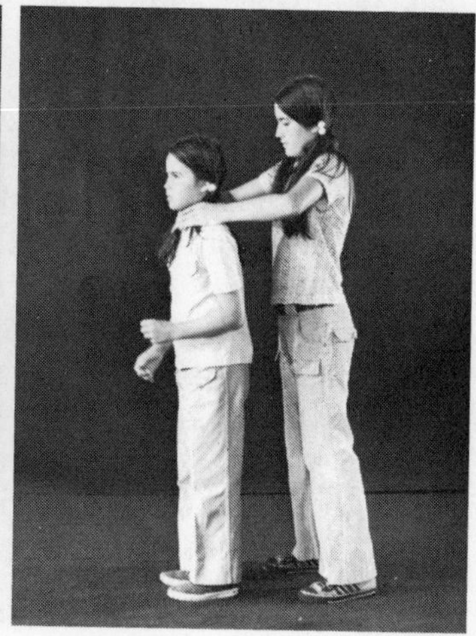

257

258

259

**258.** . . . making certain that the assailant partner's fingers are gripped firmly . . .

**259.** . . . and the release is simulated in a spirited manner and completed with a kick.

To ensure safe practice, instruct the partner playing the role of assailant to release quickly and avoid resisting the finger-bending defense. To demonstrate the effectiveness of the finger-bending release, an adult can simulate a choking grip (do not dig your fingers into the throat!) and allow the release to be done slowly. Make certain that the child experiences the feeling of success by applying a grip no stronger than would be used by an assailant of reasonable size. The point I am making is that a six-year-old child could not use this defense against the full strength of an adult, but that any nine-year-old child could use it effectively against a twelve-year-old bully.

(In unrehearsed demonstrations, it has been used successfully by a small, 112-pound woman against a strong, 200-pound man resisting as hard as he could. It is one of the most effective release defenses possible for small individuals.)

**Use the Photos**

Let the photo illustrations help you teach. Before you supervise the practice of each technique, let the child (or children) study the photos carefully, as you explain the sequence of actions. Then, if you repeat the same instructions as they rehearse, they will be following your verbal cues and remembering the photos.

260. With both wrists gripped, from the back . . .

261. . . . the defending partner simulates a kick into the shin . . .

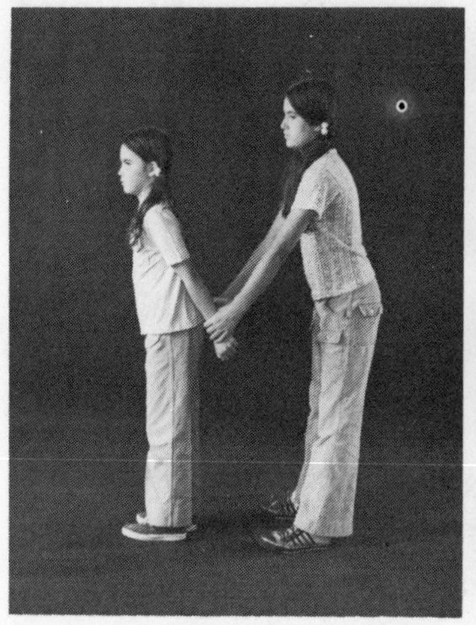

260

261

262

263

262. . . . and effects release by thrusting both hands out in front of her . . .

263. . . . and turns, ready to continue, if necessary.

After the child has practiced this several times, study the photos again, together, as a way of fixing the procedure in her mind.

Among children, as among adults, there are different kinds of intelligence. These different kinds of intelligence require different methods of teaching. The child who can watch a process and reproduce it immediately exhibits a different kind of intelligence than the child who quickly grasps instruction in oral or written form.

You might need to demonstrate the defenses yourself for the child who has sight-comprehension and you might need to read aloud to the child who requires verbal instruction.

264

265

Make as many explanatory remarks as your child wants or needs.

**264.** But, at least, explain why it is ineffective to counter strength with strength. The child being held, could not hope to effect release using her lesser strength against the superior strength of her adversary.

**265.** Using the going-with principle, she takes a step toward her assailant, putting her off guard. She grips her own captured fist . . .

266. . . . and effects release.

I have successfully taught children working together as partners and I have taught children working with adults as partners. In the past, I have had greater success working with two girls as partners and two boys as partners rather than using boys and girls together. This is not due to an inherent inability of boys and girls to work together to learn self-defense, but is the result of poor environmental models.

In working with children, the important factors are not the sex or size of the practice partner as much as the attitude of the assisting adult partner. If you cannot find a suitable partner, who is approximately the same size as your child, you could take the role of assailant partner. If you do it with tact and consideration, it is a perfectly acceptable procedure.

Be patient. Be supportive. Helping a child achieve self-reliance and self-confidence is a very rewarding experience.

# PART SIX

## THE JOLLY BULLY

Any act which has the effect of demeaning the person on whom it is performed is aggression. There are some such acts which could hardly be classed as assaults, but which are, nonetheless, hostile. Friends may engage in rough-and-tumble horsing around which is not aggressive if they have equal status in these games. But when one person always plays the role of aggressor and the other person is always the butt of the game, the victim, though he might not suffer hurt, suffers embarrassment and shame.

The assertive person does not permit these acts to be forced upon him. It is much easier to prevent them than you might imagine. If, by your tone of voice and your attitude of conviction, you can order the aggressor to stop, you are fully in command of the situation. If, however, you have been the butt of this sort of horseplay over a long period of time, you probably need the backup confidence of knowing how to handle the bully if he does not respond to verbal direction.

The physical actions which are used in these situations must be appropriate. It should be apparent that karate-punching the friendly bully or throwing him onto the ground would be wildly inappropriate. It is not necessary to "defeat" this individual; it is sufficient to demonstrate your ability to cope efficiently and determinedly with his hostile behavior.

267

268

269

270

**The Hand Squeezer**

267. He is gripping your hand and does not respond to a verbal request to let go.

268. Extend your middle knuckle and grind into the top of his hand.

269. Or, grip one of his fingers and lever it away.

270. Or, using the bony edge of your forearm, grind onto the bony part of his forearm.

If he is persistent and stubborn, you might slash onto the forearm and/or kick into the shin to complete the action.

**The Leaner**

271. The leaner is always bigger than you are and he puts body weight behind this annoying action. Tell him to stop. Or, duck down slightly and take a step back as you tell him to stop.

272. Or, dig your extended knuckle into his side, just below the last rib.

271

272

273. Or, grind your heel into the top of his instep.

**The Shoulder Puncher/Back Slapper**

274. If he does not respond to your instruction to stop doing this to you . . .

275. . . . you can slash his arm with as much vigor as is needed to convince him that you are serious.

**Butt Grip**

276. Dig into the back of his hand with your extended middle knuckle . . .

277. . . . and when you feel his grip loosen somewhat, wheel about with a snappy action, slashing his arm as you turn. This should effect release and in most instances would complete the defense.

278. If necessary, use a hand blow to finish.

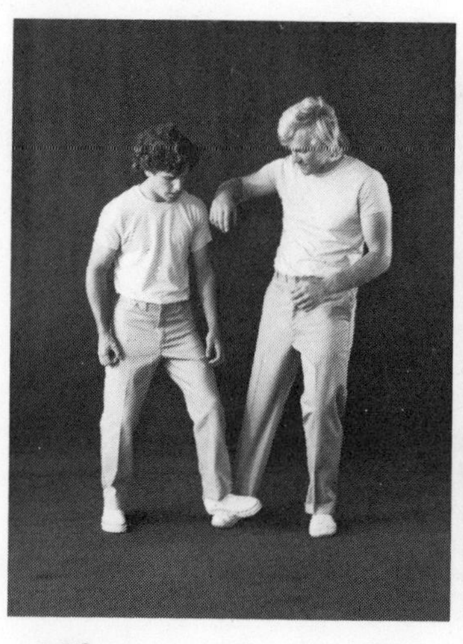

273

274

275

276

277

278

279

280

281

282

**Bear Hug**

279. You are captured in a strong grip; he digs his chin into your backbone and digs his knuckles into your breast bone.

280. As you grip one of his fingers, kick into his shin . . .

281. . . . and scrape down his shinbone as you pull outward on his finger . . .

282. . . . to effect release.

## RELEASES & ESCAPES

By now, you should be familiar with my argument *against* learning defenses as a rigid series of movements to be memorized and practiced without variation. Flexibility of response is a great advantage; rigidity of response limits the use of defense actions.

Learning a specific, unvarying defense for each specific assault is restricting because of the number of defenses you need to learn, but also restricting because you are dependent on the assailant to make his assault in a specific way.

There are, however, a few exceptions to the general principle of flexible response. For some fairly common types of grabs, holds and captures, you can learn specific defenses which are the most efficient.

If you practice the response to threat of assault, if you make your move before you are captured, if you are ready to go into action before a hold is taken, you should not find yourself in the situation of being pinned, choked or held. But, you should practice these escapes so that you will know complete self-defense.

Partners must use the tapping signal for release from holds and must release instantly upon getting the tapping signal!

**RELEASES FROM WRIST GRIPS**

Wrist grip releases do not rely on strength. Partners should demonstrate to each other how ineffective it is to attempt to struggle free by pulling away. Unless the person who is holding you is not as strong as you are, you cannot free yourself in this manner because you are working against the strong line of his grip.

283. Your wrists are gripped.

284. You begin the action by pushing outward, slightly, with both your arms. His automatic response is to push inward.

285. Using his inward push to assist your action, bring your arms sharply inward and then up and out. In this way you effect release from between his thumbs and forefingers, the weakest part of his grip.

Against a moderately strong grip, you could effect release with arm action alone. Against the grip of a very strong individual, you would start the escape by kicking sharply into his shin, once or twice. After hurting and distracting him with kicks, you effect release as described.

283

284

**Two-Handed Grip**

**286.** Your wrist is gripped with two hands.

**287.** Make a fist of your captured hand and reach over and between his arms to grip your own captured fist.

**288.** Begin the release action with a jerky, downward action; then use his reaction to snap your arms up and away.

Against the grip of a strong person, you would have to precede the release with a sharp kick (or two) into his shin.

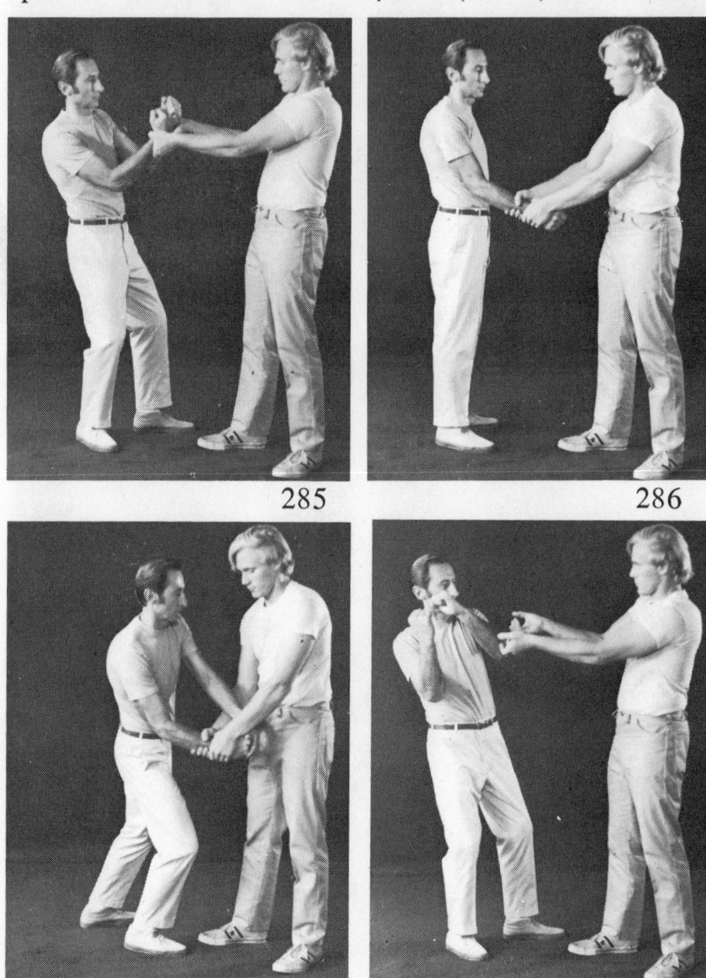

285 286 287 288

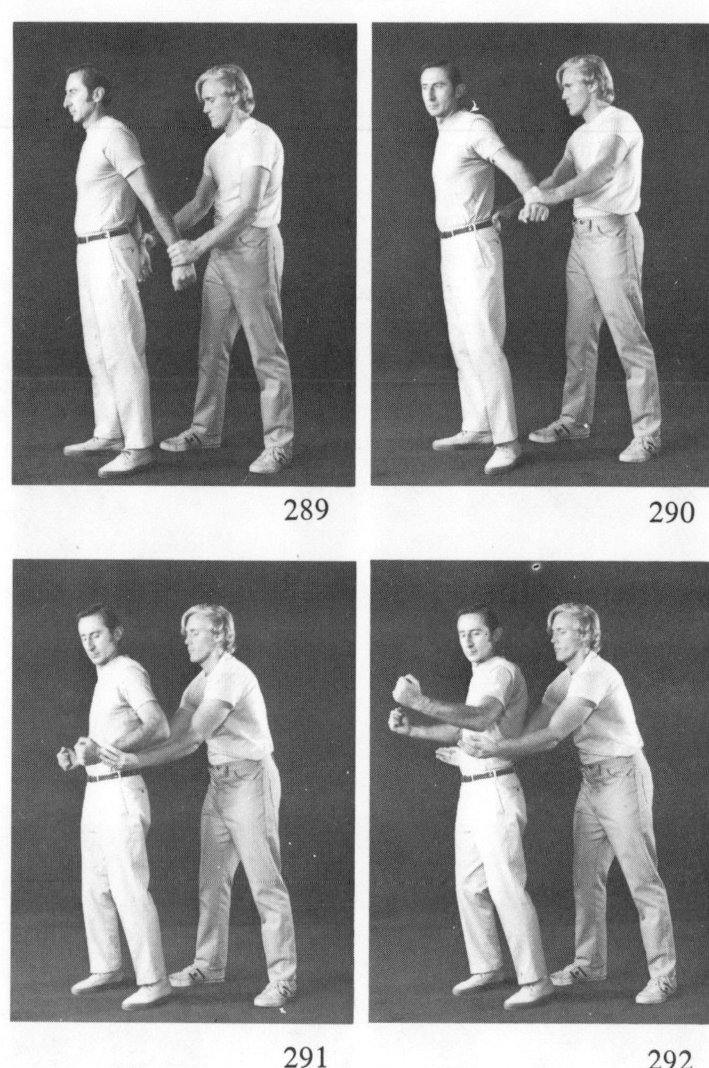

289 290

291 292

**Rear Wrist Grip**

**289.** Your wrists are gripped from behind.

**290.** Start the release action by pressing outward, with both your arms. You will feel a reaction pressure, inward.

**291, 292.** Using his inward pressure to assist your action, jerk your arms inward and then up and out, to effect release. Against the grip of a considerably stronger person, you might have to start the defense by kicking back into his shin, once or twice. When he has been hurt and distracted by your kicks, you effect release as indicated above.

### Arm Twist Release

Don't try to exchange pain for pain! If an aggressive action is being used against you and the result is pain—stop the pain first before you attempt escape.

**293.** You are being held in a firm grip, your arm is being twisted.

**294.** Reach around and grip your own captured hand and twist in the opposite direction, using both arms to twist and using body action to assist the twist. This will not effect release, but it will counteract his action and relieve the pain.

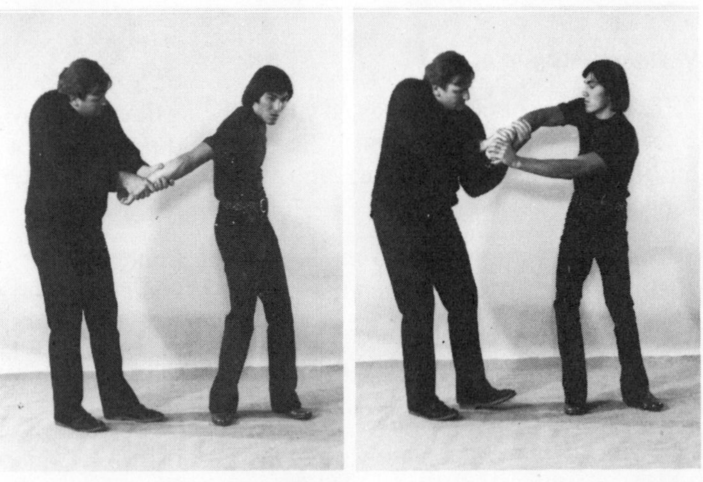

293 294

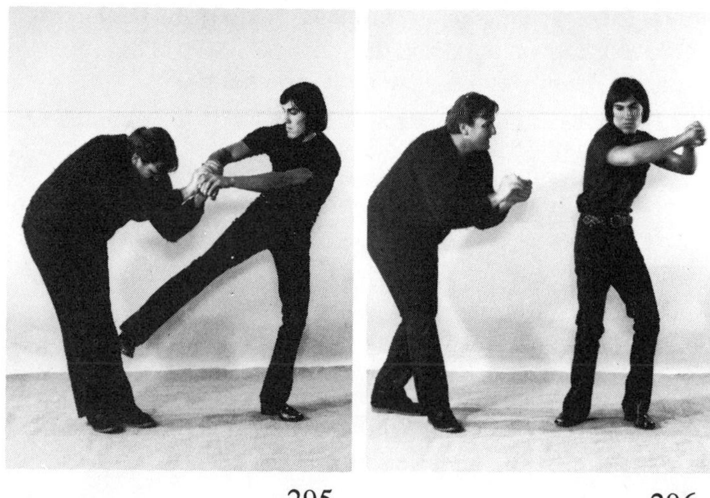

295 296

**295.** Maintain your grip and continue the twisting action; kick into the knee or shin with as much force as necessary.

**296.** When you have hurt him with the kick and feel his grip relax somewhat, snap your captured arm free with a vigorous motion.

### Yoking Arm-Pin Release

**297.** Your arms are pinned and you are being threatened by a second assailant (not shown). The man holding you is not hurting you; he is restraining you. You can use him for support.

**298.** Kick vigorously into the legs of the front assailant, continuing as necessary to hurt him enough to make him back off.

**299.** When you have driven the front assailant away, kick into the shins of the man holding you, and . . .

**300.** . . . scrape down with the edge of your shoe . . . and stamp onto his instep. Repeat this action as necessary until you feel his grip somewhat relaxed.

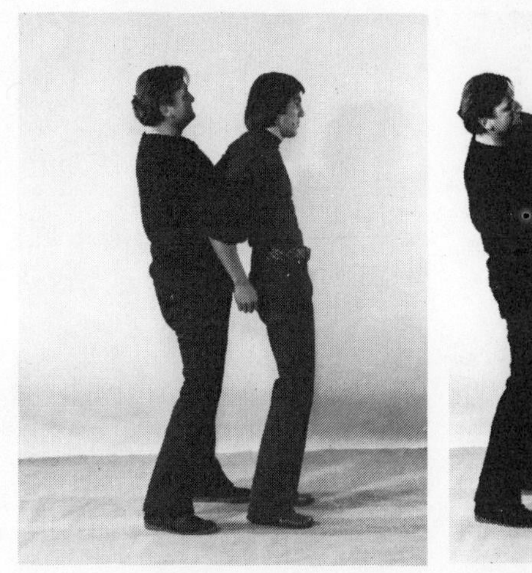

297

298

299

300

301

302

**301.** Then, twist your body sharply around to one side. This action will result in one arm becoming more firmly pinned, but it will loosen his grip on your other arm. Try this action alone with your practice partner and you will feel that the free arm is the one on the side to which you turn. In the photo, the defending partner is twisting toward his right side and it is, accordingly, his right arm which is more free.

**302.** With a rapid, thrusting action, pull the free arm upward, hitting up with your elbow.

**303.** When you have released one arm, spin out in the opposite direction to free your other arm. Hit and kick as necessary.

303

**Release From Back Arm-Pin**

**304.** Your arm is pulled up your back.

**305.** The first action should relieve the pain; reach back and grip your own wrist or his wrist and push down to counteract the pressure.

304

305

306

307

306. Maintaining your counter-pressure, kick back into his shin, vigorously.

307. When you have weakened his grip by kicking, spin around, clockwise to effect release. If necessary, use hand and foot blows to complete the defense.

### HEADLOCK RELEASES

#### Release #1

308. You are captured in a front headlock, as shown. Grip his arm at the wrist and just below the elbow, to relieve the pain and pressure.

309. Maintaining your hold, kick into his shin.

310. Repeat the kicks until you feel his grip relax somewhat. With a vigorous, jerky motion thrust his arms away . . .

311. . . . as you back out from under his grip and kick, if necessary to complete your defense.

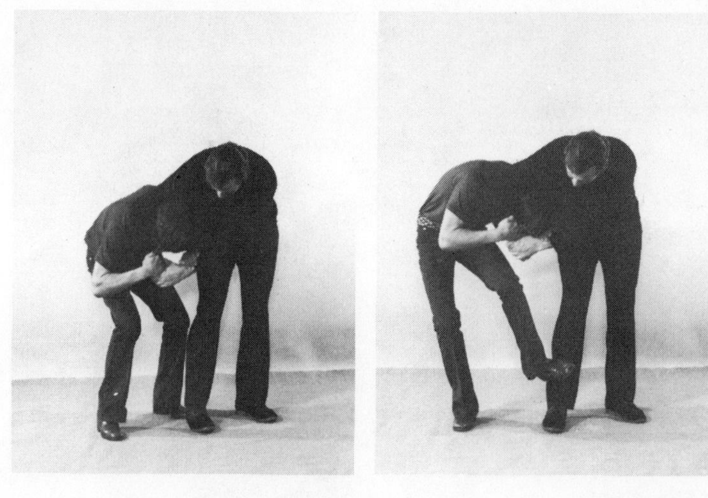

308 309

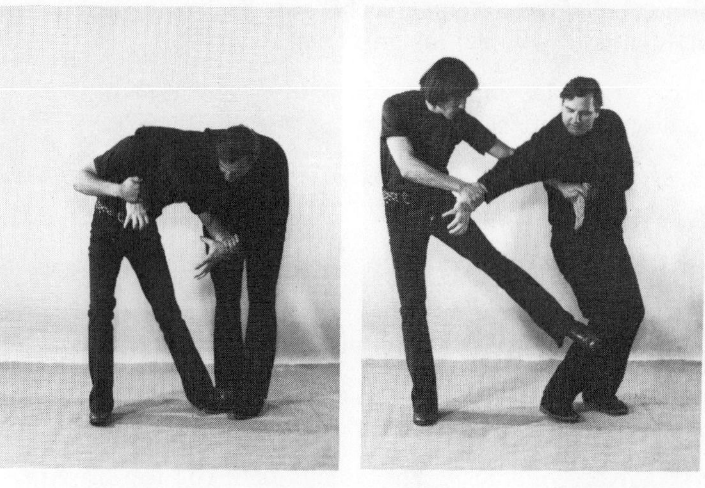

310 311

312

313

**Release #2**

312. You are captured in a headlock, as shown; grip his arm with both hands, one at his wrist and one just below his elbow; pull down to counteract his grip. Kick with vigor into his shin until you feel his grip relax somewhat.

313. When his grip is weakened, thrust down sharply with your arms to effect release.

**FULL NELSON RELEASES**

**Release #1**

314. You are held in a full nelson.

315. Relieve pain and pressure by putting your clasped hands at your own forehead and pushing back.

316. Kick vigorously into his shin until you feel his grip relax somewhat.

317. When you feel his grip weakened, thrust your arms out and down, with a sharp, quick motion to break his grip . . .

314

315

316

317

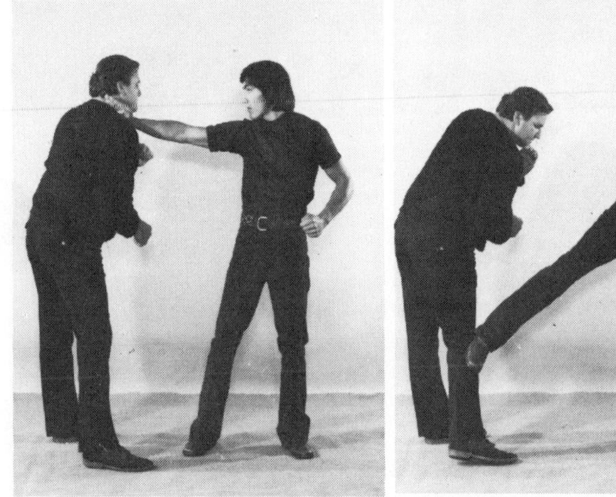

318

319

318. . . . and turn around to face your assailant, ready to complete your defense with hand . . .

319. . . . and foot blows, if necessary, to complete your defense.

**Release #2**

320. You are held in a full nelson. First, relieve the pain by placing your clasped hands to your forehead and pushing back; kick into his shin.

321. When you feel his grip relax somewhat, because of your kicks, sidestep . . .

322. . . . and place your left knee behind his right knee . . .

323. . . . wheeling your upper body counterclockwise as you thrust your left arm vigorously outward, and push with your knee at the back of his knee.

You can effect release with a vigorous arm movement and slight knee pressure, or you could wheel around with enough follow-through and a vigorous blow at the back of his knee with your knee to put him on the ground.

320

321

322

323

**FOREARM CHOKE: Mugging Defense**

324. Defending partner is pulled back off balance by a forearm choke. Partner who applies the choke note: You can take a firm grip on your partner by clamping your hand onto his shoulder and placing your other hand over it to secure your grip. Apply *very light pressure* at his throat, just enough to simulate the gesture of the assault.

325. Defending partner: Tap for release if your partner applies painful pressure at your throat. You need not be hurt while practicing this defense. Grip the choking forearm with both your hands, one at his wrist and the other just below his elbow. Turn your head into the bend of his elbow to reduce choking pressure. It is critical that you begin your defense with these two actions. Reduction of pressure against your windpipe is crucial to your defense.

If you do not relieve the pressure at your throat, you are in danger of losing consciousness.

If you try to defend by using hand or arm blows, you are vulnerable to the choking pressure. If you struggle to stand upright, you *increase* the choking pressure. You must reduce the choking pressure before you do anything else!

Pull down on his choking arm, putting all of your body weight behind this effort.

Maintaining the firm grip on his arm, kick forcefully into his shin with the edge of your shoe; scrape down along his shin and stamp onto his instep. Repeat the kick-scrape-stamp until you feel his grip relax slightly.

Obviously, you are not really going to kick, scrape and stamp, but simulate these actions with spirit. Assailant partner, react *as though* you had been kicked and stamped.

326. When his grip is slightly loosened, maintaining your firm grip on his arm, *back out* from under his arm . . .

327. . . . using one or two additional kicks or stamps, if necessary, to aid your escape . . .

324

325

326

327

328

329

330

**328.** . . . and when you are free, continue to step around behind him . . .

**329.** . . . still gripping his arm . . . which you can pull up behind him . . . or you can push him away . . .

**330.** . . . or you can complete the defense by kicking into the back of his knee for a take-down ending.

## ON THE GROUND

Prudence, caution and preventive defense will minimize the possibility that you would be caught unaware and allow yourself to be put in this position. Nevertheless, you should be able to cope with assaults on the ground.

### Pin Escape.

331. You are pinned. There is a possible range of aggressive intent in this situation, from friendly horsing around to hostile humiliation to serious assault. It will help your defense action if you talk quietly to your assailant, to calm yourself and distract him.

332. Draw your feet up close to your buttocks.

331

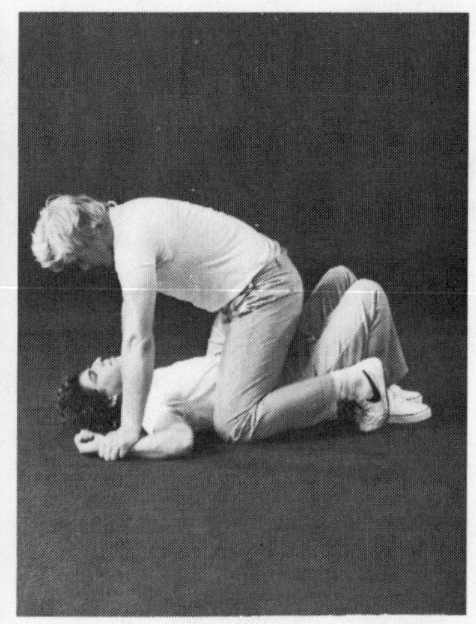

332

333

334

**333.** With a sudden, lunging action, bridge up with your feet and your buttocks. If you are considerably smaller than your assailant, you will not be able to bridge to the extent shown in the photo, but you can bridge enough to make the next action effective.

**334.** Thrust one leg forward and wheel your body in the direction of the extended leg, using your braced, bent leg to help push . . .

335

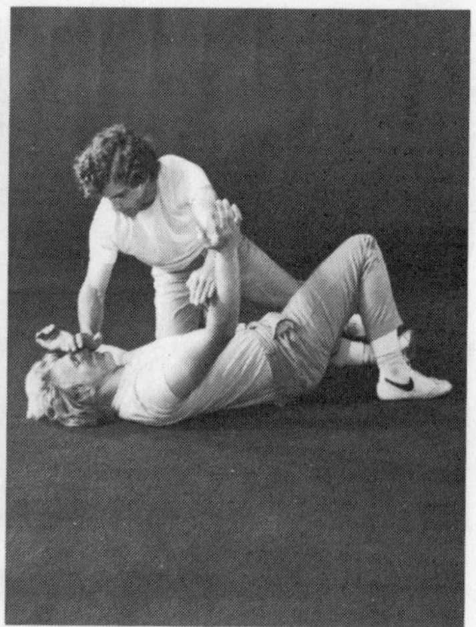

336

**335.** . . . him over and off . . .

**336.** . . . allowing you to escape. Back away from him and rise when you are out of reach of his arms and legs, or use hand blows to complete your defense before rising.

**Choke**

**337.** You are being choked; your hands are free. You can use vigorous slashing blows onto his forearms.

**338.** Or, you can use the clasped-hand thrusting action up between his arms.

**339.** Following with hand blows into his face and neck. If necessary, use the bridging pin escape.

**Punching**

**340.** You are pinned and your assailant starts to punch.

**341.** Block or parry his arms . . .

**342.** . . . and use appropriate hand blows into his face or neck.

Complete your defense by using the pin escape if necessary.

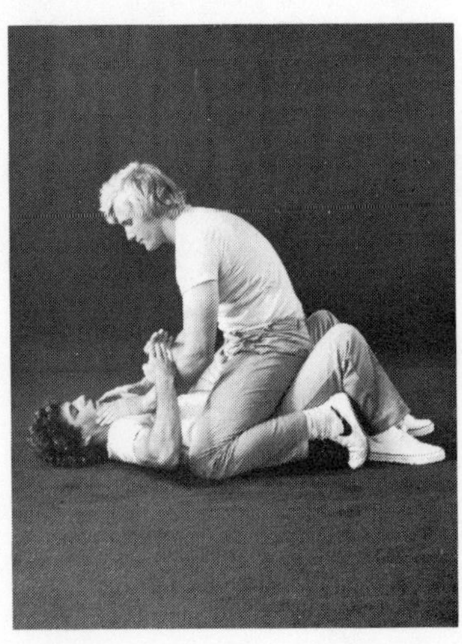

337

338

339

340

341

342

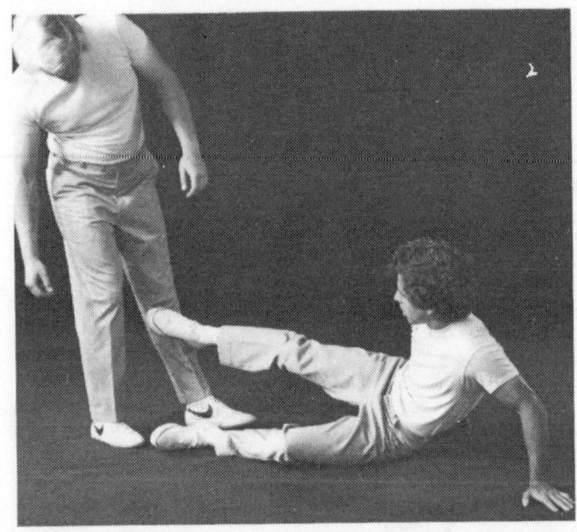

343

#### Kicking Defense

343. You are on the ground and your adversary intends to kick you. Put your body weight onto your hands so that you can swivel freely on your buttocks. Kick at his shins, vigorously. Don't let him get around near your head.

Practice procedure. Partner playing the role of assailant—be very careful not to come within range of defending partner's kicks. The procedure is practice to avoid letting your adversary get into position where he could kick at your head or into your side. As he attempts to move around to avoid your kicking action, swivel to follow him so that your feet are pointed at him.

#### Rising from the Ground

344. When you rise from the ground, stay out of range of your assailant's hands and feet. Don't make this mistake! You are safer on the ground, kicking him, than rising as shown.

345. As you start to rise, scoot back out of kicking range, facing him . . .

346. . . . and rise to a guard position.

Avoid this error.

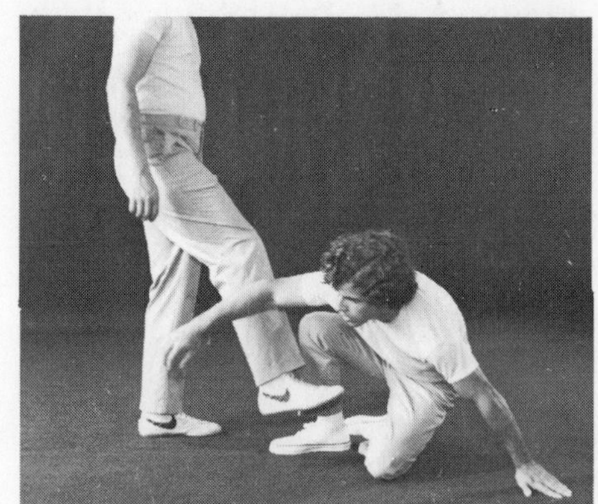

344

345

346

## DEFENSE AGAINST KICKING ASSAULTS

### Toe Kick

347. The assailant draws his leg back in the obvious gesture of starting a toe kick.

348. The most effective defense is a counter-kick into his shin.

349. Complete your defense with hand blows or any other appropriate action.

### Knee Kick

350. The knee kick is a forceful blow which is difficult to counter, but relatively easy to parry. As you side-step to move out of the direct line of his attack, slap-parry his knee vigorously, using a one-handed or two-handed parry . . .

351. . . . to deflect the blow and turn his body. Because he is on one-point balance, you could move him around so that he has his back to you. Complete your defense with a kick into the back of his knee or any other appropriate action.

347

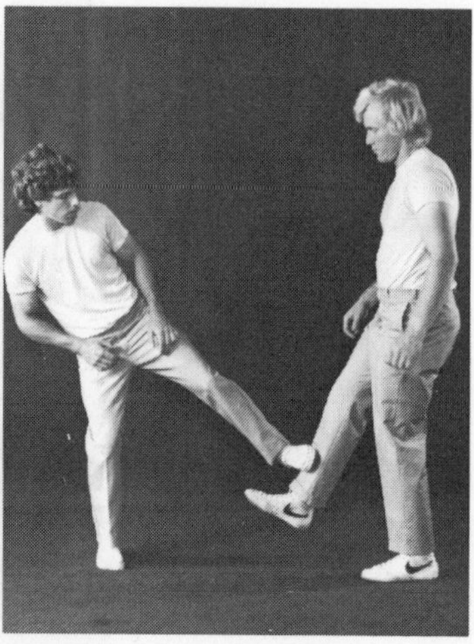

348

349

350

351

352

**352.** Parry a high stamping kick in the same manner as you would parry a knee kick. Side-step as you parry. A vigorous slapping parry could turn him completely around.

## STICK WEAPON ASSAULTS

The most effective defense against a stick, or similar rigid hitting object, involves moving in, to stay out of range of the weapon. This is one of the very few instances in which a defense is safe close in. Obviously, you would not move close in to defend if you could escape without resorting to physical action.

The two most common ways of using a stick weapon are: outside swing and back-handed swing. The defenses are similar.

### Outside Swing

353. The gesture of the outside swing is very broad—there is no mistaking the style of the assault. As the attack begins, move in close and block his hitting arm—*not* the weapon—with both your arms. The forearm block, shown, is effective; you could also use slashing open-handed blocks . . .

354. . . . and, without hesitation, grip his arm with both your hands, extending your arms rigidly to immobilize his arm briefly; kick into his leg . . . and . . .

355. . . . finish with a takedown, if necessary, to complete the defense.

353

354

355

356

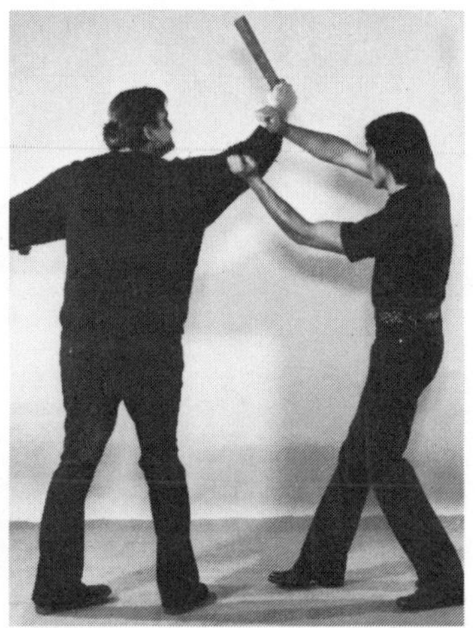

357

358

359

**Back-Handed Swing**

356. The gesture of the assault is easy to read. The stick (or similar weapon) is held cross-body, ready to swing back. Step in and to the outside of the hitting arm and block the arm—*not* the weapon—with both your arms, using your fists, as shown, or double slashing blocks . . .

357. . . . or double forearm blocks . . . and immediately . . .

358. . . . grip his arm with both your hands and extend your arms rigidly to immobilize his arm for the brief time necessary to . . .

359. . . . complete your defense with vigorous kicks.

Practice the defense against the two kinds of stick assaults, first as separate actions, and then practice them as a combination in which the assailant misses at his first attempt because you step *back* to avoid the first swing and then step *in* to defend against his second swing. If your partner swings back-handed the first time, step back to avoid it and be ready to step in for the defense as he begins his outside swing. If your partner swings outside at the first attempt, step *back* to avoid it and then step *in* to defend against the back-handed action. Be very careful with your partner to avoid getting hit with the stick. It is safest to work with a padded stick.

**Surprise Assault**

There is another kind of stick or blunt instrument assault which is greatly feared—being hit from behind. The best preparation for coping with that kind of assault is to be alert if you are in any kind of situation in which it might occur. If an assailant does actually leap out, unexpectedly, and strike from behind, there is very little you could do about it, but you *can* minimize the possibility that it might happen.

If you are alone in an area which provides hiding places for an assailant, which might as easily be a pleasant "nice" neighborhood with sheltered, dark walkways and trees as it might be a "bad" neighborhood with alleys and doorways, be alert! Be aware of sounds, shadows and movement which could clue "danger." Don't keep your back turned to possible assault; turn to face any threat. Caution and prudence will be your best protection. There is no such thing as being absolutely risk-free, but you can reduce risk by being aware of it, ready for it, and responding to signs and signals of possible assault.

Practice of the response to threat of back attack will help prepare you to cope with this situation.

### FLEXIBLE WEAPONS

A flexible weapon, such as a chain, belt, etc., is used with the same kinds of gestures as the back-handed and outside-swinging stick attacks, but the movement of the weapon suggests that the defense be made *only* when the weapon is in the back-handed swinging position.

360. If you attempt to move in close while the chain is swinging wide, it will hit you as you make your defense. Watch for the assault to begin and step or leap back as it comes toward you and . . .

361. . . . as it clears you and before he can start the reaction swing, move in . . .

362. . . . and block his arm, with both your hands . . .

363. . . . and grip his arm; extend your arms rigidly to immobilize his arm for the brief time required for completing the defense with kicks, as necessary.

360

361

362

363

## KNIFE ASSAULT DEFENSES

If a knife or other weapon is used for intimidation, and the primary intent is robbery, not assault, do NOT attempt a defense. It is reckless and foolish to risk injury to protect property or money. *Any* defense against a knife assault involves some risk of being cut, though the defenses I have selected involve the least danger of injury. These defenses should be used if the assailant intends to use the knife and that is his primary purpose.

If you feel that being cooperative and quiet will prevent the assault, the prudent action is quiet cooperation. If the only two choices you have are passive submission to being knifed or making a defense, make a spirited defense.

Grappling with or gripping the knife or trying to disarm the assailant is dangerous. The traditional aikido or jiu jitsu defense against knife assault is very difficult except for those with a high degree of skill. The most efficient defense is that which deflects the intended assault without making you vulnerable to the most serious cutting actions.

### Close-In Knife Threat

With sufficient attention to the preventive procedures of defense, you should be able to avoid being cornered in this manner. If you know how to cope with this kind of threat, you should be able to deal with it in a more prudent, calm manner, thus minimizing the danger. The knife-armed assailant expects his intended victim to betray helplessness and panic. Individuals have calmly talked their way out of frightening situations. DO NOT ATTEMPT A DEFENSE if the knife is being used as intimidation only.

364

365

**364.** The knife is held close. Put your hands up immediately and talk to the assailant. Tell him you do not intend to oppose him if he is not going to hurt you. Mean it!

**365.** If you judge that he is going to cut you if you do not attempt a defense, start with a *subtle,* slight eye or hand motion to distract his attention, briefly. Before doing this, you have noted which hand holds the knife because you are going to thrust his knife-holding hand cross-body.

366

367

**366.** Parry his knife-holding hand cross-body with a vigorous, snappy action as you thrust your hand toward his face. In practice with your partner, simulate the thrusting action, but be very careful not to make contact with his eyes! In actual defense against a knife-wielding assailant, you would be justified in using eye-stabs as part of your defense.

**367.** Grip his arm with both your hands and stiffen your arms to immobilize his knife hand for the brief time needed to complete your defense with vigorous, forceful kicks into his knee.

Do not attempt to wrest the knife away unless you are certain he is not going to struggle; if you have hurt him or put him on the ground, you might be able to disarm him without danger to yourself, but if you can escape without disarming him, do it!

368

369

**Stabbing Threat**

**368.** Note which hand holds the knife. You are safest if you make your first move to the *outside* of the knife-holding hand. Distract by talking to him and/or shifting your feet and body; keep your eyes on him so that you are ready to move . . .

**369.** . . . when you see him starting toward you; leap to the outside of his knife hand, or take a deep step outward . . .

370

371

**370.** . . . and slap/parry or slash/parry at his arm and kick into his leg.

**371.** Without hesitation, grip his arm and extend your arms rigidly to immobilize him for the few seconds necessary to complete your defense with vigorous kicks into his leg or the back of his knee.

Your defense is kicking; gripping his arm and holding it away from you minimizes the possibility of getting cut. Your relative positions in this defense also minimizes the danger of cuts into your midbody, face, or throat.

### DEFENDING AGAINST MORE THAN ONE ASSAILANT

The large, heavy person who attempts to assault a smaller, apparently vulnerable person, is not brave; neither is the individual who assaults in a group. When two or more assailants gang up on an intended victim, they rely on the understandable fear experienced by the threatened person to force him to play the role of passive victim.

When confronted by multiple assailants, assuming that you could not escape or get help, there are two possible choices: submission or a spirited attempt at defense. There is no certainty that you could successfully defend yourself against two, or three, or four assailants, but there *is* a certainty of getting beat up if you are passive.

The unexpectedness of a spirited defense effort in the face of unfair odds is, in itself, disorienting to the assailant group. There are three good tactical procedures for dealing with multiple assault. The one you use would depend on the situation.

The first choice tactic is to concentrate on the leader of the group. If you can determine which of the gang is the leader, begin your defense actions against him. The gang does not attack with the idea of getting hurt themselves and if they see their strongest member being hurt, they are likely to become demoralized.

If you cannot determine which is the leader, or if he is out of range, concentrate on the nearest individual, hurting him as much as you can without getting within reach of the others.

The third tactic is to move from one assailant to another, using hand and foot blows against them with vigor, spirit, noise and determination. It can work!

## AFTER THE BOOK

Many people who have studied with me through my books have written to ask how they might continue practicing after finishing the work outlined in the lesson plans.

What you do to maintain or enhance skill after studying from the book will depend in a large measure on your attitudes, your goals and your feelings.

### Maintaining Functional Skill

For maintaining basic skill, it is only necessary to review the techniques occasionally. If you feel comfortable with the fundamentals of self-defense, and have no special or specific need to engage in on-going practice, there is no reason why you should.

If, after finishing the work in the book, you do not feel confident of your ability to use basic, functional self-defense actions, REPEAT the course. Do not attempt to learn additional material. It is more efficient to use a small group of defense actions with relative ease than it is to try to learn many techniques. If it is difficult for you to respond with a few actions, it will be even more difficult to try to recall a great number of actions. Practice the fundamentals over and over until you feel comfortable and relatively confident of your ability to use them.

## CHOOSING A SCHOOL

If the idea of developing skill in one of the weaponless fighting specialties is attractive to you, just for exercise, it does not make any difference which specialty you learn, as long as you enjoy it.

If you live in a community which has a school, visit it, observe a class in session and then you can decide whether or not the teacher suits you. If there is more than one school, visit them and compare. You are the best judge of what is best for you even though you do not have any technical background. You are equipped with a more important gauge for making a decision—your own reaction to what you see!

Any reliable school or teacher will allow you to observe at least one complete session before you make up your mind. Verbal explanations of what is being taught are not enough; you have to see what it is. Nor should you allow yourself to be dazzled by what the teacher himself can do. You are not paying to see him perform; you are paying him for what he can teach *you* to do.

When you observe a class, watch the teacher and watch the students. Does the teacher actually instruct? Does he give clear directions and explain what is to be done, or does he merely demonstrate and leave the students to imitate as well as they can? Is the teacher patient and does he encourage the students, or is he cross and rude to students who need correction or help?

Do the students seem enthusiastic about what they are doing? Do they appear to be helpful to one another? Is there a friendly atmosphere?

Is the material being practiced what you think *you* would like to learn?

If you like what you see, the school is right for you. If you don't like what you see, the school is not right for you, even though the teacher, the material and the method might be quite acceptable to other individuals.

DON'T SIGN A CONTRACT unless you are absolutely certain that you understand what you are signing and that it is a fair contract. Unless you are familiar with contracts, you may need help in deciding whether or not the contract protects your consumer rights. If you sign a contract without reading or understanding it, you may find yourself obligated to pay for lessons you don't want to take or you may find that you cannot get a refund in case of emergency.

As a general rule, you are better protected if you make partial payments as you go along than if you pay for a full course in advance. If you make partial payments, then, if you change your mind or lose interest, or move, you are not tied to an arrangement which might be a financial burden.

If you need help in deciding if a contract is fair, if a financial arrangement is fair, or if the operator of a school is reliable, ask your local Chamber of Commerce or your librarian to direct you. Most communities have agencies which offer free advice and guidance in these matters.

It is your money and your time which are being spent. You have the right to spend them the way you please and to make sure that you will get your money's worth.

## KARATE

Karate, which is practiced in many stylistic variations, is essentially the skill of using hand (and arm) and foot blows.

Although there are many different names for the different styles of karate, there is more similarity among them than there are differences.

Traditional karate training has the objective of producing an extremely high level of proficiency. The two main divisions in karate are described as "hard" and "soft." The hard style emphasizes strength and power; the soft style emphasizes development of speed and accuracy. All styles and all schools of karate utilize similar hand, arm and foot blows.

A karate blow is not more "deadly" than a boxing blow of equal force. It is not the *style* of a blow which determines impact force; force is a function of speed/strength/accuracy. Years of intensive training result in superior ability; stylistic mode is of negligible significance.

Characteristically, karate techniques are practiced with many repetitions to achieve considerable skill for each specific hand or foot blow. When the fundamentals have been learned, students then practice formal series of pre-arranged actions in solo performance (these are called forms or dances); they practice two-man forms and they engage in free-style practice. Free-style practice is contest-like fighting.

Some schools of karate emphasize the practice of one-man forms, some emphasize one- and two-man forms and other styles emphasize contest training and prepare students for tournament.

Photos 372-384 illustrate a portion of a typical karate one-man form. In this particular form, the movements are executed with snap and speed. The transition from one action to the next is rigidly set. Students are graded on their ability to perform the movements in the correct sequence as well as for technical skill.

372 373 374

375 376 377

378 379 380

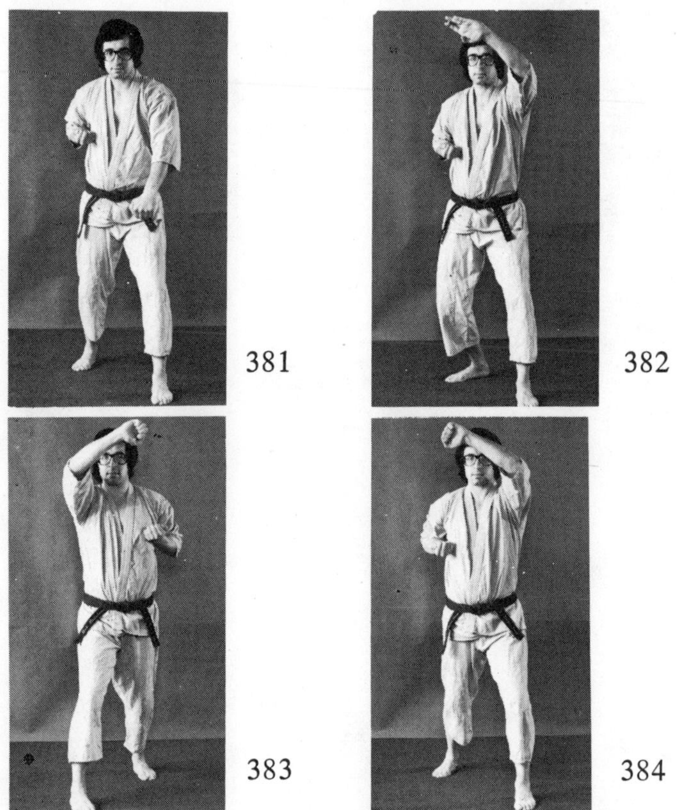

381 382

383 384

**KUNG FU**

Kung fu, or gung fu, is the Chinese form of karate which preceded the Japanese style and was derived from an even older style of weaponless fighting developed in India.

Kung fu, savate, Tai boxing and kenpo karate have elements in common, even though there are stylistic differences among them. They all utilize hand and foot blows. If one were to observe some of the techniques of karate and kung fu as pure technique, all performed by a single individual without identifying apparel, then unifying elements would become obvious.

Photos 385 to 391 illustrate some characteristic gestures of kung fu. Photos 385-388 show a typical salutation series. Photos 390, 391 are two movements from a form.

385 386 387

388 389

390

391

## JUDO

Judo is a sport, regardless of what is said to the contrary. It is played by rules and regulations; it has judges and referees; contestants of approximately equal skill are matched in play. Though there has been a tradition of teaching judo as though it were useful for self-defense, it was clearly not the intention of the originator of judo. Dr. Jigaro Kano developed judo for physical education.

The principal technique of judo is throwing; throws are roughly categorized as arm throws, legs throws, body throws and sacrificing throws. Although every part of the body is involved in effecting an arm throw, the principal, critical action is done with arm movement and the same is true of the leg throws. Body throws are those in which the opponent player is taken over the body of the thrower; sacrificing throws are those which place the thrower on the mat as the throw is applied.

The second aspect of judo play is grappling. Holds and locks are applied, sometimes in a standing position, more often on the mat and the grappling techniques are also referred to as mat work. The holds and locks bear some resemblance to wrestling, but are stylistically different and the rules of judo mat work are not the same as wrestling rules.

Blows struck with the hands or feet are not permitted in judo. The safety rules of play prohibit hurting the opponent player in order to apply a throw. Although outsiders view judo as a spectacular activity with a high risk of injury, when judo players are trained in falling safely and when the safety rules of judo are scrupulously observed, judo is not a dangerous sport.

There are so many systems for awarding belt ranks in judo (and in the other specialties) that it is not possible to describe the level of skill or to know what the player has achieved unless one knows the school or system in which the belt rank was earned. Even within one system, there is considerable variation among clubs in the method of awarding belt ranks. Since no school or system recognizes the validity of colored belts awarded outside of its system, a belt rank has significance only within the system in which it is awarded.

In the past, the colored belt ranks of players were used as a means of matching contestants for tournament. This is not a satisfactory method because of the wide variation—from school to school and from teacher to teacher—in the systems of awarding belt degree ranks. In Olympic Games procedure, players are matched through elimination events and by weight classes. This method insures better matching than matching by belt rank.

**392.** This shows the beginning practice position for a hip throw which is a basic training technique seldom used in contest. The thrower will lever his opponent player over his body.

**393.** The leg-hip throw is a contest technique favored by short players.

**394.** Tall judo players tend to favor leg throws; the completion of one such throw is shown here.

Judo is a close-contact sport and is enjoyed by people who like body-contact contest and vigorous, competitive physical activity.

392

393

394

**AIKIDO**

Aikido is a fairly recent adaptation from a specialty of Japanese hand-to-hand combat. It is stylized applications of techniques related to holds and locks. Pressure and/or twisting actions are used principally against finger, wrist, elbow and shoulder joints.

Aikido practitioners claim that many years of study and practice are required for the achievement of enough skill to use aikido for self-defense. The complexity of the techniques call for perfect timing and precision if they are to be applied successfully against a moving, resisting assailant. Years of study and never-ending practice is a condition which does not conform to the realities of most people's lives. For this reason, alone, aikido is not a practical or rational form of self-defense, in my opinion.

Because serious injury could result from resistance to the aikido techniques, practice has evolved into a non-resistant form. The person on whom the techniques are being performed does not oppose the twisting or bending action, but moves his body to follow it, rolling gracefully onto the mat to avoid the painful pressure. The stylish rolling actions seen in aikido practice do not represent actual, normal responses to sudden, painful pressure applied to a joint. An assailant not trained in aikido would not roll out of the hold to relieve the pain.

397

398

Early books on aikido described it as so ''deadly'' the masters of aikido were sworn not to reveal its secrets. Like the secrets of other forms of specialized fighting, the secret of aikido skill is revealed to be — practice, practice, practice!

Photos 395-400 illustrate the traditional garment worn for aikido practice—the hakama—and some characteristic movements and gestures of aikido.

399

400

**Games & Sports**

Being in top physical condition is not a prerequisite for functional self-defense, but there is another sense in which physical fitness and physical ability is important for people who have problems which relate to physical contact and self-image.

If you experience yourself as ungainly, inept, awkward and physically unattractive, you may very well benefit from physical activity which helps you overcome that negative self-image. I am not suggesting that you must be strong or handsome or beautiful or an outstanding athlete in order to realize a state of genuine acceptance of your body as a satisfactory part of your total self. What I am suggesting is that you work to overcome negative attitudes.

If you experience yourself as clumsy, engage in an activity which develops grace. If you experience yourself as physically inept, engage in an activity which develops physical skill. It need not necessarily be related to self-defense. In fact, I have observed significant improvement in students who diversified their physical activities. This is especially true of those who do not enjoy contact sports of competitive games. Swimming, bicycling, hiking, walking and other such physical activities can be a route to body self-esteem for many who need to improve in that direction.

If you have a child who is timid, not especially well-coordinated, either large or small in relation to chronological age, and who seems ill-at-ease in a body sense, non-competitive physical activity might prove more beneficial than traditional karate, kung fu or judo.

## GUIDE TO STUDY

The basic lesson plan which follows is intended as a guide and should be adapted to your individual needs, aptitudes, interest and available time. Use the index to find subjects and techniques. Because of the flexible-response method, you need not learn a large number of specific defenses in order to develop efficiency. For basic self-defense, practice the few actions until they are well assimilated and can be performed with relative ease. Because this handful of actions can be combined into a great many defenses, there is emphasis on creative combinations. Flexible applications of a few defense actions is the basic concept of this method.

## BASIC LESSON PLAN

LESSON ONE: Read the book, with special attention to Safety in Practice. Discuss goals and concepts of basic defense. Look at the photos. Practice: Hand blows and kicks; where to hit and kick. LESSON TWO: Blocks and parries. Response to front reach. Review practice of hand blows and kicks. LESSON THREE: Wrist grip releases. Response to back threat. Review lesson two. LESSON FOUR: Review practice of lessons two and three. Practice simple combinations using techniques from previous lessons. LESSON FIVE: Practice side-step and kick; ready stances. Practice on-going defense and complete defenses with all techniques previously learned. LESSON SIX: Review responses to front reach and back threat. Practice releases and escapes from grips and holds related to your individual need. LESSON SEVEN: Practice defenses against chokes, front and rear; defense on the ground; coping with humiliating situations (hand squeezer, back slapper, butt grip, etc.) LESSON EIGHT: Spin arounds and back takedown; knife assault defense; practice complete combinations using all material previously learned. LESSON NINE: Defenses against kicking; six-count practice procedure; quick response from ready stances. Review releases and escapes from grips, holds, chokes. LESSON TEN: Defenses against stick and flexible weapons; more than one assailant. Select specific defenses throughout the text which have special interest or importance for you. Quick run-through of all basic technique. Re-read assertive behavior material.

### LESSON GUIDE FOR WOMEN

Because the majority of buyers of self-defense books are men the assumption is made that this book might be used by a man to assist a woman. Follow the basic lesson plan, adapting it to the specific individual. Most women do not like to learn fist blows. Women, more than men, are concerned about being grabbed and held; it is important, therefore, to put special emphasis on releases and escapes and on responses to front reach and back threat. The finger-bending release is of special importance for women.

Most women (with the exception of some professionals) do not need to learn restraints and the trips and takedowns are optional. The woman student should be encouraged to select the techniques she wants to learn and practice. Each individual has needs which only she can express. Do not attempt to coerce her to learn defenses she will not feel comfortable with. In LESSON SEVEN, substitute the kinds of humiliating situations women have to cope with.

As important as any physical defense action is the material on assertive behavior; it is the foundation of practical self-defense.

### LESSON GUIDE FOR CHILDREN

Before practicing the defenses, discuss and explain the goals of practical self-defense. Undoubtedly your children have had their concepts distorted by the popular media. Avoid the mistake of stereotyping your child in the stock sex roles. Help your child learn the defenses and the attitudes which are appropriate to individual need. There are, of course, differences, but the differences are less dependent on sex than they are on temperament and on expectations in the culture. Because of environment, boys will probably react more positively to photos of the boys and men demonstrating the defenses and girls will be encouraged by the photos of the girls and women. After the first three lessons, encourage the child to be involved in selection of practice material by looking at the photos and selecting what seems appropriate. In LESSON SEVEN, encourage the child to select the situations which seem the most threatening. Try not to impose your own decisions of what is important.

If your child elects to learn defenses against assaults you think are unlikely, cooperate! Fantasy fears are as painful and as frightening as fears of real danger. Rational arguments are not effective against irrational fears, but practice to cope with the fearful situation can allay anxiety and have important, confidence-building effects.

### LONG RANGE

A long range plan to practice self-defense techniques can have one of two objectives: you can practice to achieve a very high level of skill using the basic techniques of practical defense or you can practice to learn the greatest number of defense techniques with the widest range of applications. The objective will determine the procedure.

If you wish to reach a high level of skill using the minimum number of techniques, begin by following the basic lesson plan. When you have covered the material as outlined, start over. The second time through, take as long as you need to perfect the technical aspects of each action. Use the training aids as needed. Make as many repetitions as you can to improve technical ability. If you select optional material to suit your individual interest and aptitude, be careful to retain technical ability to perform the basic material by practicing. If you find that you lose the ability to perform fundamental techniques, you are trying to learn too fast. Remember that a high level of proficiency is maintained only through constant, on-going practice.

## INDEX

**BRUCE TEGNER** is a specialist in sport and self-defense forms of weaponless fighting. He is regarded as this country's outstanding authority, teacher and innovater in the field.

He was, literally, born to the teaching of unarmed fighting skills; both his parents were professional teachers of judo and jiu-jitsu and they began to train him when he was two years old! Until he was eight years old, his mother and father taught him fundamentals; after that, he was instructed by Oriental and European experts.

In a field where most individuals study only one specialty, Mr. Tegner's background is unusual. His education covered many aspects of weaponless fighting and included instruction in sword and stick fighting, as well. Before he gave up competitive judo, he was the California state judo champion. He holds black belts in judo and karate.

Although Bruce Tegner was trained in the traditional manner, he originated a new style and method when he began to teach. He separated and distinguished between sport and self-defense forms of weaponless fighting. He introduced new concepts for modern applications of the ancient skills.

In the U.S. armed forces, Mr. Tegner trained instructors to teach weaponless combat, he taught military police tactics and he coached sport judo teams. He has trained actors and devised fight scenes for films and TV. From 1952 to 1967 he operated his own school in Hollywood where he taught men, women and children, exceptionally gifted students and blind and disabled persons.

Bruce Tegner has twenty-five books in print in this subject field, with additional titles in preparation. Many of his previous books have been highly praised by professionals in physical education and recreation. The books range from basic, simple self-defense to exotic forms of weaponless and stick fighting for experts and specialists. Bruce Tegner's books are used for physical education classes in public and private schools, recreation centers, law enforcement training academies and by enthusiastic individuals throughout the world.